POLITICS IN AN ANTIPOLITICAL AGE

POLITICS IN AN ANTIPOLITICAL AGE

G. J. Mulgan

Polity Press

First published in 1994 by Polity Press in association with Blackwell Publishers.

Editorial office:
Polity Press
65 Bridge Street
Cambridge CB2 1UR, UK

Marketing and production:
Blackwell Publishers
108 Cowley Road
Oxford OX4 1JF, UK

238 Main Street
Cambridge, MA 02142, USA

ISBN 0-7456 0812-4
ISBN 0-7456 0813-2 (pbk)

A CIP catalogue record for this book is available from the British Library and from the Library of Congress.

Typeset in 11 on 13pt Sabon
by Photo·graphics, Honiton, Devon
Printed in Great Britain by T.J. Press, Padstow, Cornwall

This book is printed on acid-free paper.

CONTENTS

ACKNOWLEDGEMENTS

The central arguments set out in this book have developed over a number of years. Like most people I can only think in a community: in the continuous interplay, argument and parallel thought that takes place with many other people sharing similar concerns, interests and insights. In such a community ideas rarely have obvious origins or authors. They evolve rather than being invented, which makes it both difficult and invidious to single out particular individuals for credit and thanks.

This is particularly true of this book because a number of the essays contained in it have appeared in earlier versions which then received unsolicited, but often very useful, comments and criticisms.

Several first appeared in the now-defunct magazine *Marxism Today*: 'The Power of the Weak' (December 1988), 'Worlds out of Kilter' (September 1989), 'The Reimagination of the Public Sector' (May 1991) and 'The Renewable Energies of Politics' (December 1991). Although they have been substantially re-written, my thanks are due to Martin Jacques for his patience and energy in editing these into a more coherent form, and for his canny ability to mix blunt criticism with encouragement. Two of the articles have been retitled for this book.

The essay on television and quality first appeared, again in a somewhat different version, in *The Question of Quality*, published by the British Film Institute in 1990. My thanks are due to Richard Patterson for permission to republish it.

'Citizens and Responsibilities' was previously published in *Citizenship*, edited by Geoff Andrews (Lawrence and Wishart, London, 1990). I have left it largely unchanged, even though the arguments it raises have subsequently become the subject of a very lively debate.

'Reticulated Organizations' appeared under a different title in a *Political Quarterly* special edition in 1993. My thanks are due to David Marquand for commissioning this piece.

The other essays are published here for the first time.

I owe particular thanks to three individuals. My father, Anthony Mulgan, for editorial advice; my partner Helen Wilkinson for her patience in listening and contributing to the arguments as they developed, and for co-authoring one of the essays; and my former employer, Gordon Brown, both for the privilege of learning from him, and for his generosity in giving me the time to develop some of these ideas. Naturally, all the usual disclaimers apply.

INTRODUCTION

After the partition of Poland awakened the modern theory of nationalism, Lord Acton wrote that thenceforward there was a nation demanding to be united in a state: a soul, as it were, wandering in search of a body to begin life again. The same description could be applied to the philosophies of the left today: a soul of values, emotions and traditions that is now wandering restlessly in search of new bodies, new forms and structures.

This book, born not so much of the crises of 1989 as of the much longer crisis of industrial socialism, its problems of adaptation to the high modernism of new industrial structures, of societies oriented to consumption and mobility, is a part of that search. It is a search with implications far beyond the traditions of the left. For as the title essay argues, much of what appears to have been a crisis peculiar to the left really concerns what we mean by politics itself. It is a crisis which has effectively brought to an end the 200-year existence of a continuum of left and right, progress and reaction.

The thesis of this book is at once simple and complex. Its simple argument is that the socialist movement which more than any other shaped the politics of the twentieth century, through persuasion and reaction, became defined, inevitably, by the ideals of organization that prevailed when it first became a serious contender for power. As such it was imbued with the concepts of early industrial society, with its images of production, its defining metaphors and its sense of possibility and limits. Indeed, at its very heart, it shared a rationalist, progressive, systemic view of change with the wider culture.

For many decades this gave the socialist movements a huge sense of purpose and energy. Immanent in wider processes of change, it could credibly pose as the wave of the future, the true standard bearer of the future against tradition. Everything from the mechanisms of cinema, to the structures of car plants, to the evolution of government seemed to confirm the story told by the socialists.

Yet the strengths of one age become precisely the weaknesses of another. The very industrial logic which had sustained it in one era became archaic as the world shifted: as consumption took precedence over production, not only in the balance of the economy but also in its culture; as economic organization moved towards more fragmented and flexible forms; as the physical aggregations of people in cities and factories were replaced by more private and small-scale forms; and as information became a driving force less as something concentrated at the centre and more as something that flows through every pore of society.

For several decades the result was confusion, decline and intellectual uncertainty, all of which culminated in the defeat of social democracies in the 1980s and the sudden collapse of communism in 1989, precisely 200 years after the French Revolution.

That period of confusion is now coming to an end, although not in the sense of a return to the status quo ante (those who expect a reformation of the left in any recognizable form will be disappointed). Part of the reason is negative: the hugely confident right of the 1980s has retreated in its heartlands – the Anglo-Saxon countries – as its theories failed the tests of experience, first in economic management and subsequently in the public sector. It too has paid a heavy price for an overreliance on ideology rather than practical knowledge and experience.

But part of the reason is also positive. One factor is the rediscovery of the pre-industrial roots of the left, their common heritage with other movements for co-operation or equality, and the dawning recognition that many of their organizational approaches bear remarkable similarities to those of the late twentieth century. What these suggest is that, far from being a historically defined movement, finite in its relevance, the modern socialist movements are better understood as manifestations of much older traditions. Rather than being the vehicle of special interests, they are the temporary guardians of much older values, which do not fit within the French Revolution's continuum of left and right.

The second factor is the great return to ethics that has marked the last decades of the century. Again, relatively timeless ethics rather than historical ideologies have proven better starting points for politics and progress. This too has fuelled a rejection of that antimoral, hyper-rational socialism that rejected timeless moralities as intrinsically false. Instead, like its counterparts of more than a century ago, the renewed left seeks a fixed ethical position as the starting point for its critique of capitalism and injustice.

The third factor is global. The disappearance of communism in all but a few blighted backwaters has removed one of the right's most potent arguments and the fear in the hearts of all thinking socialists that Soviet communism did indeed express the essence of their system taken to its logical conclusion. The collapse of some of the old ideological anchors has been both terrifying and, for those willing to take up the challenge, liberating.

Taken together these factors explain why the left's demise has been so exaggerated. Politics is, after all, a competitive game. One side's strength makes for the other's weakness, and vice-versa. The failure of the new contenders – like the green parties which have notably failed to establish themselves as mainstream competitors on the central issues of politics, or the regionalist and new right parties – has given the old ones a reprieve.

Yet this reprieve will be useful only if it is used to pollinate, to question and adapt. Although a tradition can renew itself internally when the crisis it faces is not fundamental, it is only with an eclecticism of ideas, a willingness to beg steal and borrow from other traditions and other sources, that a tradition whose fundamental being has been threatened can be renewed.

One of the reasons why politics has become so stale and uninspiring is that it has lacked fertilization. Where in earlier times political theorists drew eagerly on the new ideas from economics or from philosophy (one thinks, for example, of the Austrians who later contributed to new right politics, or the scientific ideas that shaped Marxism), today there has been little borrowing from the extraordinary explosion of ideas around ecology and biology, the study of organizations and anthropology, the new sciences of complexity or religious ideas about responsibility.

This book offers a selection of essays that aim in a modest way to do that. They draw on ideas from biology, systems theory, history and anthropology, as well as from more orthodox sources. Some of their concepts might at first glance seem more easily pigeon-holed on the right or centre, or on the green margins, than on the left. To the extent that they succeed in contributing to a renewal of left thinking, they also hasten the demise of the definitions within which it has become caught.

At their centre, and as a unifying theme, are the problems of organization. If economics has been the dominant theory of recent decades, perhaps even of the century, it is now beyond doubt that its position is being supplanted by a broader, perhaps less sharply defined, set of theories of organization. This is probably the inevitable characteristic of information-based societies, where the continual application of new modes of information processing and dissemination casts attention on to structures of organization. Its interesting consequence is to throw off kilter all traditional ideologies, and to force all to address common problems such as the suppression of crime, the maximization of output or the elimination of waste. It is also an unavoidable consequence of modernity, when all institutions must be consciously created, when social reflexivity means that all are subject in their turn to conscious assessment and influence from theory, and when the enlightenment dream of man and society making themselves may have lost its lustre but is nevertheless still there as an inescapable fact.

But if organization offers, as it were, a theoretical high ground that can play some of the roles once played by a narrowly material economics, this is only part of the story. Politics is being distilled into component parts, which taken together may not add up to the coherent and consistent whole of an earlier time.

One part concerns individual meaning and identity, a problem not only for political movements that need to attract adherents by offering them a sense of purpose and being, but also for societies that are riven by competing and incommensurate identities.

A second part is the continuing question of the state, its functions and legitimacy, its boundaries of competence. Here the naïve theories of an earlier time, which saw states as nothing more than transmission mechanisms, have been displaced by their mirror: purely cynical theories that analyse states as inherently predatory and self-interested. Now the interesting questions concern how the undoubted self-interest of bureaucracies and political parties is balanced by other motivations, and by an understanding that there are roles that only states can play. So even if the presumption in favour of the state comes to seem as archaic as the divine right of kings, this will not end the argument but only put it on to a more realistic footing.

The third part concerns the evolution of global co-operative structures and a global public that is groping towards common solutions for trade, environment and security, challenging traditional notions of sovereignty but still unsure where sovereignty will be found in the future.

These essays aim to provide some of the tools for thinking about the very different world that is forming – covering everything from international relations to broadcasting, from the future of the public sector to the nature of personal responsibility. Their purpose is to provide tools for renewal, novel ways of thinking about traditional problems.

E. H. Carr once famously wrote that 'politics are made up of two elements – utopia and reality – belonging to two different planes which can never meet'. This book, by contrast, belongs to the long tradition which believes that the two are always meeting, communicating and driving into each other, pragmatists bumping up against dreams, dreamers colliding with realities. That is precisely the excitement of political life and discourse, and why even in an antipolitical age, political arguments retain an ability to inspire and repel.[1]

Note

1 E. H. Carr, *The 20 Years Crisis, 1919–39*, Macmillan, London, 1966, p. 93.

1

POLITICS IN AN ANTIPOLITICAL AGE

Permanent revolution was originally a political idea. Yet today it is more likely to be found in business and culture, or among those concerned with the shifting sands of daily life, where much of the once familiar furniture of the modern world has been thrown away. By contrast, politics has become a decidedly conservative realm. There have been few of the sudden transformations of civil war and revolution that characterized previous decades. Governments have carried on governing. Passions have cooled, and the commonplace culture of parties and parliaments, ideologies and manifestos, movements and programmes has come to look quietly solid, free from any direct threats to the paraphernalia of elective democracy, and unthreatened by any new parties sweeping all before them.

But façades can be deceptive. The apparent solidity of political structures shares less with the great religions, and more with the absolutist empires of the nineteenth century or the European empires of the interwar years: it is grand and persuasive and firmly rooted in the daily lives of millions, but it is built on foundations that have already been irreversibly eroded. For beneath the inertial momentum of elections and offices, the political traditions that became organizing principles for so many societies, dividing them into great tribal camps identified with class, with progress or reaction, with nation or liberty, have lost their potency. They cannot inspire or convince. They do not reflect the issues which passionately divide societies. They are no longer able to act as social glues, means of recognition across distances of geography and culture.

What remains is a gap, psychic as much as instrumental. Without great movements, it is much harder to understand your place in society, much harder to picture where it is going. And without coherent political ideas, to organize the fragments of many issues, fears and aspirations, it becomes far harder to act strategically and to think beyond the boundaries of individual lives and relationships. It is not that the great questions have been answered: just that the available solutions have lost their lustre.

What is coming to an end is one of the elements of modernity. Usually when we think of modernity it is to its technologies, its modes of war and communication, and its economic dynamism that our minds are drawn. Yet modernity would be unthinkable without its politics, which are as distinct from those of Machiavelli or Aristotle as the car is from the carriage. Like the industries whose rise it mirrored, modern politics is a recent creation. It began in the embryonic forms of corresponding societies, fraternities and pamphleteering barely 200 years ago in the time of the spinning jenny, the musket and absolutist monarchy. It fed off rationalism and enlightenment, the rejection of old deference, and a faith in people's capacities to solve their own problems. Since then, like the modern firm and the consumer good, the television and the jet, its world of activism, declarations of rights, organized parties, mass elections, manifestos, parliaments, constitutions and professional politicians has spread to every continent.

Like many social creations, this political world took on the character of something natural and immutable, firmly rooted in upwardly mobile, educated and assertive populations, schooled to challenge and question. Albeit in the highly specialized form of party contest, representative democracy has continued its global spread, from India to Chile, from South Africa to the Philippines, an extraordinary global reach comparable only to that of capitalist ideas and institutions. Yet 200 years on, the forms of modern politics are in irreversible decay even as they continue to spread.

In many of the most advanced and prosperous societies, the world of politics already has the feel of something archaic: a set of rituals, a container of tensions, a symbolic link with the past rather than a dynamic force in the present.

There are many morbid symptoms. In most of the democracies voter turnouts and party memberships have gradually fallen; where they have remained high, levels of commitment have fallen. Incumbent governments have tended to survive not because of any enthusiasm but more from cynicism about any available alternative. Negative compaigns have proved more effective than positive ones, and negative movements of disaffection have proved more dynamic than affirmative ones. Beyond elections, political movements have been largely displaced by life or religious movements, and movements of group identity. Youth, the traditional home of political passions, has turned away from orthodox politics towards religion, hedonism and issues such as the environment, animal rights or AIDS. With everyday faith in political solutions at a low ebb, the repute of politicians as a profession has fallen down to the lower reaches – cheek by jowl with journalists, lawyers and other systematic distorters of truth. Perhaps the most visible symptom of depoliticization is the absence of movements bringing people to the streets. The great marches are long gone. Those that do command attention are either the 'life politics' movements of environment or reproduction – creating a politics that is personal and global but only tangentially interested in the classic national political sphere – or reactionary movements to protect vested interest from attacks.

At first, the disenchantment with politics was seen as a peculiar problem for the left. It has traditionally been the most obsessively political part of the spectrum, promising political solutions and holding political participation in high esteem. But that analysis was too narrow, not least because it underestimated the extent to which the structures of modern politics are understandable only as responses to the growth of the left, and of its progressive institutions. With them in decline, much of the tension that held politics together falls away. Just as the end of global ideological struggle in the form of the cold war removed the *raison d'être* of many parties of the right, so more generally has the end of a simple struggle between progress and reaction, the future and the past, played havoc with the idea of politics. That is why it is politics more generally that is cast into question: the ideas that at one time seemed to define nations, interest groups and classes have decayed, and now, like the religions of a previous era, they face the prospect of a profound secular disenchantment.

What is Modern Politics?

To the ancient world, politics was very simple: it was what the political class did with their political institutions. It was a practical, non-reified concept, and one that clearly excluded women, slaves and outsiders. It was a world of people making decisions rather than of abstract institutions, a world where Carl Schmidt's definition of politics as about friends and foes, us and them, was perfectly sufficient.

In the modern age, politics became something quite different, a common property. For the first time ever, its practitioners claimed to the mass of ordinary people that its power, the power of the new political institutions, was the most important power, more relevant to them than magic and gods, kings and lords, more important in defining them than how they dressed or how much they earned, and more effective at bringing change than any remedies of priests, doctors or merchants.

This claim depended for its credibility on a quite new system of social communication. Its infrastructures were those organizations that involved the mass of the population in decisions and ideas: the political parties, the mass organizations, the trade unions, the lodges, the new guilds and leagues, and above all the mass media which helped to organize and self-organize the public. Modern politics is indeed properly confined to the age of public opinion – which of necessity has been an age of communications media, first of the press and later of radio and television. Public opinion was originally the preserve of a metropolitan elite, and, at one remove, of landowning interests and provincial notables. It was interrupted only occasionally by peasant revolts and urban mobs. But by the eighteenth century, with urbanization and improving communications, it had spread to a growing middle class, and by the late nineteenth century to a substantial part of the population, reached primarily through the medium of newspapers, originally closely tied to party and faction. During the twentieth century public opinion has come to include the great majority who vote in elections, are polled by pollsters, watch television and read newspapers. As they have become drawn into the political game, the forms of politics and media have continued to be closely linked. The commercial mass media which first marginalized the directly aligned media at the end of the nineteenth century pioneered new ways of covering politics, of campaigning, mythologizing and vilifying. As they did so, the older media based on relatively coherent communites and communities of interest were replaced by mass media, monologic in form, gradually transforming much of political competition into a search for the most effective powerbite, the most emotive image. Only very recently have the potentials of new technologies suggested an evolution back towards dialogic forms and the multiplication of smaller publics.

The important point, however, is that, just as the minority politics of the Greek *polis* was constituted by the communication of those gathered in the agora or plotting in factions, so too in the modern age has politics been constituted by its media of communication: the institutions like parties or trade unions, churches and leagues, the newspapers and magazines and the cultures, since it has been these that have bound political communities together, and through these that collectives have been able to think about their condition and their options.

The Character of Modern Politics

If these media and institutions formed the infrastructures for modern politics, what were its distinctive characteristics?

First, it was organized around, and in reaction to, movements for change based on class interests which saw themselves hooked into the future. These classes may only rarely have had the classical simplicity of the grand theories, but few would now dispute either that bourgeoisies (however defined) played the key role in creating a civil society and a language of rights, or that the growing power of working classes was the decisive factor behind the spread of democracy.[1] But at the end of the twentieth century, such clearly defined class interests have been eroded by changing economic, occupational and social structures, and by a loss of much of the cultural homogeneity that bound class movements together in the past. Their very success in entering the heart of the polity has denied them their earlier sense of mission, and almost nowhere is a class politics now at the leading edge of politics, defining who is friend and who is foe.

Second, politics was organized in a national arena, focused on the control of state power within defined boundaries and rules of sovereignty. Its rise went alongside that of nation states, conscious of a distinctive identity and destiny, and the goal of democratic politics was to win control of that monopoly of power within the nation that was locked up in the state. Now the pertinence of the national levels of political economy has been reduced by a globalizing economy, by localism and by the failure of national governments to solve the problems they set themselves. Indeed, although the nation clearly remains the pre-eminent political entity, it is in secular retreat.

Third, and perhaps most defining of all, modern politics has been characterized by universal transforming ideologies which have counterposed ought to is, setting up a template for judging the world, and taking universal values from philosophy into the arena of daily political contest – such concepts as freedom, equality, reason and life. Democracy is the highest of them all, a secular version of Christian theology in which the democratic power of the people replaces the will of God, and in which man becomes his own creator. Even as democracy continues to spread around the world, however, these transformative ideologies are in abeyance, submissive to the larger economic system that has prevailed, sceptical of man's capabilities as creator and seeking change by stealth rather than head-on contest.

The state of these three characteristics of modern politics, the politics of class, nation and transformation, each chipped away at the top and eroded at the bottom by the deep currents of societal change, suggests an edifice in crisis. But their decline is not a sufficient explanation of why politics might be in terminal decline and why it might be legitimate to talk of an antipolitical age or of the coming end of a 200–year era when politics has reigned supreme. Nor do they suggest how the deeper problem of social order and solidarity may be recast when political movements are no longer able to provide credible articulations, good reasons for people to cohere to others. For that we have to dig deeper, to examine precisely which elements of the political world are likely to be cast off, and which will redefine themselves in new forms.

The Decline of National Solutions

The central institution of the modern political era has been the national state, sovereign within defined boundaries, and answerable to the community of citizens within it. This peculiar historical construct reached its modern form between the end of the nineteenth century and the middle of the twentieth, and is continuing to spread in some parts of the world. As we have seen, it was at least in part a product of transforming ideologies, and a belief that the people had the power, almost the obligation, to make their world anew.

This was not lost on their governments. Empowered by democratic legitimacy, as solid a foundation as any in history, governments at first found many problems to solve: they created rational justice systems, and educational systems to ensure mobility and to help citizens play a full part in the polity. They built roads and railways and extended infrastructures of water, electricity and gas. They developed industries, standardized measurements and qualifications, and devised new symbols of community, national and state traditions suitable for an age of popular sovereignty.

Over time, however, it has become clear that such states face unavoidable structural problems. One is that their essential form – the national bureaucracy – experienced a law of diminishing returns as victories were won and barriers overcome. Each additional increment of national government seemed to deliver less tangible rewards. Every time a problem was solved, solution of the next problem seemed to benefit fewer people at a higher cost. Public action began to take on something of the character of a zero-sum game in which, as Machiavelli had pointed out, the losers are bound to be more vocal than the prospective winners. Naturally, one effect was that interest in the political process declined as governments were less likely to be convincing sources of solutions to fundamental problems.

Such laws of diminishing returns are nothing new. All empires experienced a point at whch further expansion, or further internal standardization, could be won only at excessive cost. Effective control is costly and must be used sparingly if it is not to drain the centre. Firms too face the same dilemmas. Many more things are possible than are achievable. Yet if the prevailing ideology lays great store by risk and enterprise, or by the virtues of public action, it is peculiarly hard to stick by a cautious equilibrium.

There are, of course, solutions to this law of diminishing returns. Control can be restructured, with power devolved down to agency organizations so that the state can seek the sleight of hand of siding with the citizen against the bureaucracy; local and regional government can be encouraged to take over national functions on the grounds that their equation of costs and benefits may be different. Powers can be passed up to transnational bodies which can solve problems which are insoluble at a national level. All of these are sensible steps. But all inevitably save the national state only by diminishing its *raison d'être*. They save political concern only by parcelling it out among different institutions and communities. And none rescues politics from that impotence described by Hans Magnus Enzensberger as world politics comes to 'resemble repair shops where worried mechanics are bent over stuttering motors and scratch their heads pondering how to make their jalopies work again'.

Underlying this problem of diminishing returns is the cost of monopoly. The rise of politics paralleled the rise of the state: what had been a lean body, concerned primarily with security and the minimal regulation of trade, grew voraciously in the nineteenth and twentieth centuries. The spread of its technologies

of governance, the means of knowing what citizens did, of regulating them and defining right conduct, has been the greatest
single change in the political order, right up to the end of the
twentieth century. In the prosperous societies, the state has come
to account for between a half and a quarter of all wealth. In
exercising such economic power, government has been based on
an implicit theory, the theory of sovereignty according to which
power can be concentrated at a single point, held by a single
monopolist at national level, in marked contrast to the divisions
of power of the medieval era (which is why one pope described
the concept of *raison d'état* as the Devil's reason). Originally, the
monopolist was the king or emperor. Democracy simply passed
over the sovereign's monopoly of power to the people, and in
practice to the state which acted in their name.

As such, politics, which entered the modern age as the agent
for the self-definition and assertion of communities, became
locked into the logics of the state, well described by Nietzsche
as the 'coldest of all cold monsters'. Politics became a contest for
state power, for power over the machine, even as that machine
quite clearly shaped the nature of the political entities that fought
over it. In Michel Foucault's words, because of the ability of
states to transform themselves into governments with tentacles
reaching throughout society, 'the problems of governmentality
and the techniques of government' became 'the only political
issue, the only real space of political struggle and contestation'.[2]

Yet the monopolist of power could never monopolize solutions:
it could never live up to its implicit promise, and it could never
prevent a disillusioned reaction. The retreat from faith in a monopolist state, bearer of a single rationality, had a paradoxical
effect on politics. While formal politics became ever more locked
into the concerns and practicalities of government, antipolitics
grew in parallel, with democratic impulse transformed from its
association with integration and nation to become the force of
resistance to systems, of movements that pioneer new social
themes against the orthodoxy, of personal salvation against public
stultification.

While antipolitics has spread on the margins, monopolist
national states have also faced a permanent point of pressure

through the politics of taxation, appropriately since in Edmund Burke's words, 'the revenue of the state is the state'. In certain respects this crisis of the tax relationship represents only a new chapter in an old saga. Contrary to Marxist assumptions, the classic political revolts were all sparked off by tax, that is to say by conflicts between states and peoples rather than between classes. Whether against the Romans or the Abbasids, or in the Peasants' Revolt, the English Civil War, the American War of Independence or the French Revolution, the motive of revolt was in each case the excessive demand of first the imperial and later the national state, usually seeking to sustain its overweight military machine and bureaucracy through legal extortion.

One of the characteristics of modern politics is that it has transformed the logic of taxation and thus of the tax relationship. Whereas throughout most of human history tax was a tool of elites beyond any accountability to their citizens, in democracies tax, although individually compulsory, is collectively dependent on consent. Instead of those at the very top using tax for their own ends, tax becomes one of the tools for using the wealth of the rich to benefit the majority through social security and pensions, railways and schools, health and jobs. It becomes one of the means of democracy, a mechanism for organizing common wealth. But as is the case with national states, so too in the case of tax is there some evidence of a law of diminishing returns. At a certain point each increment in taxation to fund a public activity begins to provide net benefit to fewer people, until a minority becomes dependent on a majority. This happens only at a very late stage. Only since 1945, and the huge expenditures and moral consensus of war, has the burden of taxation substantially included the majority through income tax. For most of the decades since then the 'deal' of higher taxes and higher common services seemed reasonable.

Yet however legitimate it may be, tax remains an inherently unpopular thing. For most people it is one of the few purely coercive relationships, with no right of appeal or exit. When it raises tax every state is absolutist. Whereas in other spheres of life modernity has brought choice and transparency, in governmental revenue raising and spending these are rarely present. And so, as the majority comes to support a minority, a minority that does not work or that lives elsewhere, democratic arguments have gradually to shift from the strong ground of collective interest to the much weaker ground of collective philanthropy. The lesson of recent decades – from the time of California's Proposition 13 and Norway or Denmark's Progress Party – is that this shift is not easy to make.[3] It depends on a sense of community which the steady substitution of state for community, itself central to the political mission of the last two centuries, has rendered inadequate. The result is that there is no sufficient common morality or language for the majority to fill the benevolent roles of the traditional rich. Put cynically, the tax revolts do no more than show up politics for what it has become, no longer an offshoot of organic communities, no longer a grand mission to build heaven on earth, but rather a demand for money by a predatory bureaucracy and its political allies.

What this analysis suggests is that the tax crisis is inseparable from a wider crisis of public ethics, and that this in turn is inseparable from the way in which politics is structured. Where in an earlier era politics could more easily claim a moral fervour and righteousness, this is much harder when it has become so deeply embedded in a system of governance. Where radical politics was once rooted in the interests of civil society, today it revolves around the decision needs of a complex system of national and local government.

One of the extraordinary features of modern politics is the extent to which is has become formalized as a game of government and opposition, generally with a degree of rotation. Political movements become governments in waiting and, almost by definition, once in power, oppositions in waiting. Issues are forced into binary form, for and against, with the general public organized into binary armies, ready, at least where the big issues are concerned, to follow the agreed line.

Such binary opposition has some historical precedents – most famously of all in the greens and blues of ancient Byzantium – but by and large in the past such divisions have been associated with civil war and temporary schism, lasting only until one side achieved undisputed hegemony. What is peculiar about the modern system is that a binary system is institutionalized not only in the forms of parliamentary life but also in the media which structure reporting and argument into binary forms.

This politics is the very antithesis of the transformatory idea on which, as we have seen, modern politics was formed. It renders politics less significant, less valid as something in which to invest too much time or too many hopes. It assists in its professionaliz-ation and diminishes its attraction for participation. And despite offering an unprecedented stability in which to organize varying interests, it carries an immense ethical cost, in that politics loses the capacity to question the system of which it is part.

Politics is Bypassed as Life is Elsewhere

If the various structural problems facing national states go some way towards explaining why politics has lost its charm, there are also more general explanations. One popular one is that the programmatic, transformative politics of modernity has been beached like a great whale carried by an apparently unstoppable tide. While the parties and parliaments went on talking, what had previously been non-political issues became the great matters of life, the real issues by which people defined their position in the world. Some of these issues, such as global warming or the spread of AIDS, are by their nature macrocosmic and worldwide in scope, and so beyond the realm of practical politics. A new politics of the species, of life and of global interconnection drifts easily into mysticism. Others, in the microcosm, are intensely personal, concerning identity and purpose, battles over sexuality or home life, neighbourhood and culture, and the unprecedented quantity of decisions forced on individuals and institutions with-out the guidance of tradition. Much the most important of these has been the empowerment of women, which in the space of a few generations has posed a radical challenge to the traditional forms of politics and to political classes that are still unclear just how fundamental a threat they may face.

Perhaps the biggest challenge is that both sets of issues, the macrocosmic and the microcosmic, are soluble less through the passing of laws and decrees than through changes of culture and behaviour. Sovereignty, the monopoly power of violence and law, becomes impotent and even foolish in the face of such a challenge, since the soft realms of culture are beyond the reach of its rigorous and hard laws. Traditional politics has, as it were, been left stranded between the two, the macrocosmic and the microcosmic. It carries on with a momentum of its own, the massive inertia of great parties and career ladders, but finds itself ever less able to resonate or to provide satisfactory sanctuaries for people's hopes and cares. Its power is no longer the power that people feel is most important. In Ulrich Beck's paradoxical words, the effect is that 'political modernisation disempowers and unbinds politics and politicises society'.

In some senses, as this suggests, the weakening of formal politics is a hallmark of a wider success. For politics to have become bypassed it was first necessary to take political modes of questioning and argument into all realms of life, making the narrowly political less special as a result. Because modern democratic politics makes people the creators of their own worlds, it requires them to question and contest, to build according to their own reason and not that of any higher being or any inherited belief. Such contestation and questioning of fundamental categories has spread far beyond politics and into personal life, sexuality, eating and dressing, economics and academia. Just as every individual creates him or herself, so does every institution have to redefine itself, and justify itself anew. No institutions are in this sense apolitical: all are subject to democratic questioning, to faction and argument.

This is quite a special meaning of politics, but it is one that has slipped into ordinary use. Politics becomes a sensibility more than a set of institutions, an attitude for probing domination and inequities. Even conservatism becomes highly political, contesting everything from the contents of TV programmes to the behaviour of public figures. Nothing is assumed, and indeed everything assumed is suspect, since it can be assumed only because of a hidden power lurking behind it. In this sense, politics becomes less part of the definition of the collective, the nation, class or republic, and more part of the armoury of the self-defining, self-creating individual, continually required to make decisions on everything, including what to eat, where to work, and what relationships to maintain with friends, relations and children. It vanishes from the committees and parliaments because it has gone everywhere, into the bedroom and the kitchen, the workplace and the bar.

Politics Disempowers

The third theme is the idea that the means of politics – the meeting, party and resolution – gave more opportunities for the average individual to influence events than any other. Its openness and its demotic styles encouraged the participation of all. Yet right from the start a very contrary view persisted. First, there was the idea that an active state precluded an active citizenship; at the very least there was a tendency of substitution as professionals came to substitute for classes of people, particularly the poor and the sick. Politics became professionalized, the 'ordinary person' ever more of a rarity, the person of standing who used to enter politics as a sideline replaced by the career politician, and rule by oligarchy established in even the most democratic movement. At worst, states simply sucked up the political realm into their administrative decisions, transforming citizens into passive consumers of decisions who could legitimately distance themselves from responsibility for the effects of their actions or from responsibility to solve problems themselves.

Second, there was the argument, articulated with growing stridency since the 1940s, which counterposed the openness and, ironically, the democracy of the marketplace with the closed and unequal world of politics. The market, it was claimed, is open to all; it makes no demands of status or class, of connections; it is open not simply to those with the peculiar talents essential to political activism, and it is transparent where real politics is opaque.[4]

Third, there was the more subtle notion, that the media–politics complex, that axis at the centre of most advanced democracies, had disempowered electorates through its organization of opinion and debate. The media and politicians would propagate opinions, test them through opinion polls, and thus recycle them, newly legitimated, into the political world. A closed system of opinion formation, opinion legitimation and opinion consumption by government seemed to exclude a sovereign electorate except at rare moments, when the public would resolutely reject conventional wisdoms expounded by the media–politics complex, moments which would be experienced as ones of extreme crisis. Politics thus turned into a sophisticated system of disempowerment, whose very rituals of openness became mechanisms for legitimating decisions made elsewhere.

These explanations are symptoms of the decay of something more fundamental, the very founding myth of modern politics, the myth that all can participate equally in decisions, a myth that Schumpeter traces to the Christian belief that the Redeemer died for us all and that he 'did not differentiate between individuals of different social status'.[5] Democratic societies treat this principle as sacred: the old idea that some were better placed – by background, education, property or some spurious notion of morals – to make decisions, was long ago rejected as a crude cover for narrow interests.

Yet politics is an activity undertaken by relatively small numbers of people, primarily professionals in the parties, government, media and consultancies. These producers of politics shape the range of issues and questions, the available alternatives, and the conventional wisdoms about what is feasible. Naturally, they have to remain open to change in the wider society, to movements which spring up in the regions or suburbs, to bitter anxieties and radical hopes that arise as if spontaneously. But to the extent to which the professionals are good at their jobs, these are all susceptible to being co-opted, managed, taken account of. The result, in Niklas Luhman's cynical words, is a gulf which 'separates the ethics of face to face interaction from social requirements in say economics, politics or services' so that 'moralistic demands for more "personal participation" in social process are hopelessly out of touch with social reality'.[6]

The cynic therefore has a simple and powerful argument. If there is oligarchy, however open at the edges, why should the general public go through the motions of participation, sanctifying and legitimating decisions over which they have little say? Why should they not tire of the myth, become adult and see it for what it is, a modern species of the magic Malinowski analysed among the Trobriand islanders, an attempt to give the appearance of control over important events which are in fact uncontrollable? Was it not inevitable that they should at some point reject that huge weight of ideology that makes them feel that they should participate, should understand exchange rate management or weapons reduction, should live a public life, when in fact it is only in private life that they are really in control?

Clearly, many people do continue to participate, even when objectively the great majority are powerless. But they may do so more from a desire for self-esteem than from rational conviction, just as in many societies the poor take part in rituals of role reversal even though they know them to be charades designed to divert social antagonisms and strengthen the grip of the powerful. If so then it is not a move away from rational engagement, but rather an ascent into rationality that makes people lose faith in the political myth and gradually disengage, to use the political power of occasional elections only negatively, to remove the bad, to keep out threats and interference.

Giving weight to these ideas is the fact that since the middle of the twentieth century, and perhaps since Nietzsche, it has been popular to believe that history has come to an end, and that the great transformations are all to be found in the past. The world is stagnant, exhausted, locked into closed loops of bureaucracy and culture that exclude new energies. In such a world no one is in control, and therefore no one is worth opposing or overthrowing. All important decisions are locked into systems – those of finance and money, of bureaucracy, of culture – which are themselves mutually isolated, rendering radical change across spheres all but impossible. In the words of one perceptive German writer, 'the rulers have ceased to rule but the slaves remain slaves'.[7] The dominance of systems gives good grounds for avoiding politics. If power is no longer exercised by people who can be identified and called to account, most political action will amount to little more than tilting at windmills. The development

– societal and individual – promised by modernity becomes a chimera.

Philosophy Devours Politics

Each of the reasons I have suggested for the demise of modern politics and the rise of an antipolitical ethic has been buttressed by the more abstract arguments of philosophers. To situate these it is necessary to recall that the age of modern politics began with a full-scale reconceptualization of how politics should be considered. Where previously it had been understood as a set of techniques for statecraft written in manuals such as those of Lao Tsu or Machiavelli, in the modern world it became umbilically linked to the philosophies of enlightenment and reaction from which it had been born. As such, it brought with it great stories of human progress to replace the older religious stories of redemption and judgement. Sovereign man may in theory have been his own author but in practice he (and it was almost never she) took his stories from a handful of masters. They provided stories of the rise of reason, the conquest of the old and the accumulating domination of nature and the progress to utopia.

Many of the stories cast politics in a central role, providing the arena for the decisive battles that would usher in a new society. Philosophy provided a sort of fuel for politics, a ready stream of concepts, arguments and images for the enterprising political activist to popularize. Founded on apparently solid philosophical principles, political beliefs and programmes could be situated within grander schemes promising consistency and coherence across philosophy, history, economics and psychology. They could be legitimated by connection to theories of human nature, great sweeping tendencies of human history.

Buffeted by ideological excess, the twentieth century has not been kind to such stories. The grander the story, it seems, the grander have been the unintended consequences. The greater their claim to intellectual coherence across a range of fields, the less has been the likelihood that any ideology will survive unscathed. So it is that most modern philosophy refuses to accept responsibility for such grand schemes, preferring to analyse, deconstruct or debunk excessive claims. It distances itself to a cold, often hostile criticality, where ethics is reduced to a tolerance of other world-views, 'respect for the other as what it is: other',[8] and where the role of philosophy is always to challenge the conventional understandings and meanings, to be instinctively against rather than for. This need not imply a complete detachment. In Foucault's words, it is not that everything is bad, but rather that 'everything is dangerous',[9] and that consequently the philosopher's role is not to distinguish the good from the bad, the rational from the irrational, but rather to warn of unseen dangers that lurk in apparent rationalities and benevolent intentions.

The old claim to coherence and consistency has been replaced by a more modest sentiment: at the limit the view that each sphere of life, whether philosophical reflection, political action or economic management has its own quite distinct knowledges and practices. The implication is that political claims should be able to stand on their own two feet, justified by their own types of logic and by historical experience, not by overblown claims and illegitimate borrowings from other fields.

Shorn of support from the philosophers, and with no apparently firm ground on which to stand, no solid founding principles, politics has had to return to the more complex ground of ethics and to the craft of managing divergent interests. It has become just another part of the permanent change that characterizes modern societies, subject to perpetual innovation and adaptation (rather than the construction of an enduring system) and constant demands to choose. It has fallen prey to that undermining of essence that afflicts culture and belief more generally.

For some the heart of this problem is the question of virtue. At the beginning of the industrial era, politics was self-consciously informed by a sense of classical origins, of civic virtue in which political participation was a virtue in itself. Active engagement in the political life of the society became a ready source of approval and of self-identity. Those who were apathetic, usually the vast majority, were regularly berated: the 'hidebound, inert and dormant' masses in Lenin's words, the 'cold indifference of the masses, their willing slavery' in the words of the Chartist

George White. But the virtues of participation were shared not only by the transformers but also by moderates for whom it was deemed part of the bonding of a healthy community, even if, as J. A. Pocock showed, many worried about the compatibility of classical notions of civic virtues and the personalities needed to succeed in a civil, trading society.

Republican traditions in eighteenth- and nineteenth-century USA and in Europe clung hard to a belief that politics should be about community rather than interest, co-operation rather than competition. Some sought, as did Hannah Arendt in this century, the re-creation of a political class of active citizens at the core of such a community, and a society of direct discussion[10] and face-to-face democracy. Instead, however, detached from any theological foundation, ideas of virtue have been eroded by acquisitiveness and by the substitution of state for community, a general characteristic of modern societies. Media and physical mobility have diminished face-to-face social intercourse, while the replacement of life for system in all spheres appears to have bred detachment from, and cynicism about the public good. The economic system, as was feared, rewarded grasping and selfish personalities. Later, prosperity tended to undermine the work ethic which had previously provided the system with its driving energy, an insoluble cultural contradiction at the heart of capitalism.

This erosion of virtue, which Alasdair MacIntyre associates philosophically with Nietzsche, and historically with the disappearance of the social forms in which virtue and the common language of virtue can flourish,[11] threatens any ethical politics. It makes politics little more than a balancing of interests, devoid either of any mission or of any overarching criteria of judgement, leaving no reason for anyone to care or to take part.[12] Those who are ethical and virtuous in their approaches to politics, such as Gandhi or Martin Luther King, can be so precisely because of their distance from the political game rather than because of any possibility of virtue within politics.

Hatred of Power

The various arguments I have set out all concern the problems
faced by ideas when they encounter the real world. They are all
problems of power: problems of a world era when humans are
irretrievably collective in their forms of social life, interdependent
and interconnected, blessed (or cursed) with a huge power over
nature and over each other, and brought up in cultures that tell
them that they are sovereign beings in submission to no one.
What is remarkable in retrospect is that, after the wild hopes and
disillusions, the promises of redemption and amelioration, we
still lack a realistic account of power that is appropriate to a
democratic era. If there is now an antipolitical era dawning, and
an antipolitical ethos, it is forming at least in part because the
claims of politics and the life-forms it inhabited were fundamentally flawed and limited, and because the very political philosophies which were dominant contained within themselves an
antipolitical ethic.

Both classic liberalism and Marxism were in an important sense
hostile to politics. Where the former sought to brush politics into
a tightly restricted corner, as at best an unavoidable evil to be
kept in a minimal state, Marxism promised to eliminate politics
altogether in an administration of things. Both contributed to an
intellectual climate hostile to power, reaching its ultimate forms
in the ideas of the 1960s and 1970s; of Foucault and Habermas,
seeking an end to all domination, and in the former case resting
in absolute opposition. Both sought to avoid the problems of
power by legislating them away: literally in the case of liberalism,
and metaphorically in the case of Marxism through the pretence
that class is the only significant source of power and oppression.

Politics, by contrast, is premised on the assumption that power
is not a thing which can be removed or even marginalized. Power
is natural to human society, as is the plasticity to make things
anew, to use power to human ends. And with power comes
domination and difference, simply because power is of its nature
dynamic, throwing up new divisions, prides, resentments and
possibilities for oppression. Perhaps one of the problems of poli-

tics today is that its proponents went silent. The most articulate thinkers about political life constructed antipolitical utopias, or criticized the world for its excess of politics. Filtering deep into the popular consciousness, these nineteenth-century ideas left a residue of distrust: a longing to believe that there is nothing natural about politics, and a strong 'anti-power' ideology, which calls for doing away with bureaucracy, industrialism and systems, so as to leave the individual alone. In its older forms as in the newer ones, such as the New Age movements and the cultures of necessarily dissatisfied youth, it represents a dramatic shift away from the idea of power as the handmaiden of autonomy towards power as its enemy.

Competitive Fantasy and Virtual Politics

My last reason is the most fundamental of them all. If true it would make it hard to believe that there is much scope for politics at all, for this concerns the very nature of the means of communication through which politics takes place.

It is a striking yet banal fact that we now live in a world in which fantasy and reality are impossible to distinguish. Information is the raw material of both fact and fantasy, and has been so industrialized that its origins are rarely visible. Now it can be manufactured, twisted, multiplied and disseminated almost without limit. Assisted by the power of computing, it can be created as if from nothing: tailor-made to cognitive needs, put together as pastiche or copy. It needs only minimal reference points. The links between it and an objective reality – the claim of positivism and enlightenment – are ever more tenuous. As a result, for the receiver there are few grounds for judgement, apart from received authority or limited experience.

In such a world it should be no surprise that fiction can seem to reign supreme: that the fantastic drives out the real, while those who master fantasy, and plug into the most effective and resonant images, become invulnerable to failures. The smile, the soft tone and the balmy phrase; the inexplicable image of positivity; the confidence that breeds confidence; the tough look of resolution; the quiet strength; all these have become the elixirs of political life, and arguably more important than a grasp of issues or philosophies. These can come later, and can be bought off the shelf. They are plentiful whereas televisual effectiveness is scarce.

We have already seen that it is no coincidence that the age of politics and democracy coincided with the age of industrialization of information. After all, such an industrialization was essential for bringing the mass of population into politics through instantaneous connection and participation, the receipt and dissemination of views. The fear now is that what was once the accessory and the means has swallowed the end. These fears may be exaggerated, for there is a larger number of people today in direct contact with complex issues, primarily through printed media, than there probably ever has been. The technicians of society, the engaged laypeople, do act as a constraint on intoxicated image. But increasingly they see their role not as guardians of politics against unreason, guardians of truth against the mobs, but rather as guardians of rationality against a politics which floats free beyond any grounding in judgement. Until the structure of the human mind or the culture of understanding changes, the media of politics, the thirty-second clip, the fifteen-second news item, the poster and the leaflet, are ruthless in imposing their grammars on what can be said.

Priests or Professionals

These limits to politics, these pressures towards an antipolitical ethic, leave us back with the old questions, for although the forms of politics are in disarray, the reason for politics remains. Societies can no longer live according to 'natural' rules, or according to inherited traditions. With an immense population, largely living in cities, human life is unavoidably collective. Decisions cannot be easily subcontracted to individuals or firms as an alternative to politics, particularly because collective security, whether from environment or warfare, remains as pertinent as ever. Nor can states easily wither away (however much they may devolve their operational responsibilities) when the public realm is in expansion.

What we are left with is a problem awaiting a solution. The inherited political movements are unable to offer either convincing ideological solutions to the problems of modern societies, or effective means of organizing social solidarity. Parties cannot avoid looking like elderly institutions that have been overtaken by more effective means of campaigning, communicating and policymaking, whether these be in the voluntary sector, the media or the research institutes. Even as they continue to be formally effective at winning elections and filling governments, they are condemned to perpetual underachievement. Even as they offer programmes, they seem less able to offer coherent frameworks for thinking about the world.

The very nature of politics is thus in a period of transition whose end points are hard to fathom. Past precedent suggests, however, that after a period of confusion and uncertainty there will be a new crystallization, at least for a period. So although the politicians of the twenty-first century will be as unlike those of today as they are different from Gladstone, Gambetta or Ulysses Grant, it is already possible to discern something of their likely character. In what follows I therefore set out what I see as the three distinct types of politican that are likely to emerge out of an antipolitical age, each compatible with the arguments made above, but each largely incompatible with the others.

The first could be described as business as usual, except that in the past the politican had at least to pay lip service to a background in a community, to an experience of 'real life'. This business as usual, by contrast, simply accepts the evolution of political action into the monopolized province of a professional and largely metropolitan elite, densely networked with the media, law and finance, living and breathing a world of power, manoeuvring, gossip and deception. Such a profession is in some respects self-contained and self-justifying. But it does have a genuine craft to offer. It represents constituencies in their various dealings. It can become a profession of brokers in a diminishing territory of increasingly minimal solutions to increasingly maximal problems. It can help the dialogue between other institutions and interests. It can clarify and resolve, dampening expectations and bringing perceptions closer to realities, and it can assist in the political presentation of non-political goals. As such it is a path already well-trodden – towards an unloved status of specialists in the arcana and craft of poll, position and image. It involves no great missions and scarcely even a vocation. But it does for all that fill an apparent niche in a complex society that is always having to negotiate with itself.

The second option would be much more radical. It would involve politicians eschewing the compromise and lack of ambition of professionalism to become instead the secular successors of priests and story tellers. Their goal, in other words, would be not to reconcile opposites but to create new unities, to create meaning where it otherwise would not exist: instead of indulging in a new polytheism, they would resist it. As such they would have to cultivate charismatic powers of leadership and become adept at the rituals of politics; redefining them but as more than empty pageant (and now backed up by the latest technologies to discover which images and phrases, which identities work and which are flat). And because positive visions are not enough on their own, they would also have to find demonic enemies to mobilize people against.

Working in favour of the priest-politicians is the fact that there are still no objective criteria for choosing leaders. Although almost every other role in society demands appropriate qualifications, leaders are still chosen according to intuitions and instincts. But because modern societies feel ill-at-ease with this fact, there is a paradoxical interest in justifying choices in the almost mystical language of natural leadership and charisma, precisely the qualities which the priestly figures can bring.

Also working in their favour is the power of television to make image override content. The picture can conjure up a sense of trust and faith more easily than the printed word. Formats can pass from the world of televisual entertainment into politics fairly easily – one reason why TV stars are becoming political leaders almost as regularly as economists did in the 1960s and 1970s. Television can also act as the bridge between charismatic religion and charismatic politics, even if politicians have a problem that few religions leaders have, namely that their miracles face the tough practical test of improving voters' quality of life in this world rather than the hereafter.

Both types of politician can work with both monologue and dialogue. The modern professional representative attempts to craft monologue to perfection, increasingly refusing any forum in which genuine dialogue is possible, and thus any common learning. He or she offers crafted parries to any attack but manages everything to constrain any scope for two-way communication, or any possibility that minds are being changed. The priest too can be just as monologic – imposing a vision or values on a passive audience of receivers. But both can also move beyond the constraints of ther own origins, to the hardest politics of all but also the most powerful – the politics of dialogue, openness and mutual learning, which requires both its technicians and its inspirers, a politics suitable perhaps for a more interactive electronic media, just as twentieth-century politics fitted the pyramidal media so well.

This leads me then to the third choice, and the most interesting: the politician as social creator. It represents a conscious rejection of the three dimensions – national state, ideology, class or interest constituency – within whose space the modern politician had to function, while at the same time remaining in tune with the most fundamental idea of politics, the expression of a self-conscious collectivity.

At its origins, the makers of modern politics got one thing right and one thing wrong. Where they were right was in believing that the world had entered a newly malleable era, when societies and individuals had to be created by their own efforts rather than with the help of tradition. The new age of chartered towns, corporations and associations with legal identities separate from the people in them reflected a society that now had to develop consciously through inventing new institutions, roles and even needs. Every institution came to be contestable, every goal up for grabs, and every day decisions had to be made using experience, analysis and theory to create new types of organization. At the same time organizations, thousands of them, filled in the space between the citizen on the one hand, and government (or God) on the other. In the words of Charles Perrow, organizations 'vacuumed up a good part of what we ... always thought of as society'.[13]

Where the makers of modern politics were wrong, however, was in believing that a narrowly conceived politics, bound up in a set of connected institutions, could become the monopoly of that power and that hope. As we have seen, the national state and national parties could not for long act as sufficient vessels for political energies and aspirations. Sooner or later these were bound to overflow. In the same way the early moderns were wrong in believing that any one ideology could generate a comprehensive and consistent set of answers to how you should run your life, the state or the relations between citizens. As a result they were wrong in believing that the ideal politican is a servant of an ideology.

By contrast, I suspect that the politicians of the future will work across boundaries, making their own coalitions, their own philosophies and their own communities. Instead of inheriting the three-dimensional model of nation-state, ideology and interest, they will have to forge their own tools. Far more than their predecessors they will have to create the environment in which they operate.

First, they will have to define their state. Where the great politicans of the past had to operate within the tight demarcations of the sovereign state, their future equivalents will not automatically seek to ascend the formal political structures of national power. They may as likely see their role as transnational or subnational, serving a diaspora or a cultural minority, or a broadly spread community of beliefs. The permanent institutions within which politics work will slowly cease to be dominated by the classic national political party. Instead the successful politician will be a broker of different types of institution, linking parties to transnational, ethical and interest groups.

As such, and given that formal representation will continue to be predicated on the assumption that the most relevant communities are geographical ones, politicians may often eschew the forms of traditional politics, acting more like entrepreneurs to create institutions and forge new relationships across geographical and social boundaries. Wherever there are public organizations, and already many cannot be fitted into national boundaries, such politicians will be present acting in the spirit of Robert Unger's celebrations of plasticity as bearers of imagination against the inertia and apparent solidity of social forms.

Second, and as a consequence, they will have a very diferent relationship to their constituencies than the politician based on interest. Theirs will be a less material relationship, less based on objectively identifiable interests, and more on communication and mobilization: shared mores and values. Their role will be to articulate this, to re-energize it, and their driving ethos may be transcendental, derived from the interests of the species as a whole, as much as from more prosaic interests. What will make them representative and legitimate will not be election so much as their ability to define constituencies and common interests, representing them to others and to themselves, and bearing all the hallmarks of politics except the formal ones.

Their third characteristic will be ethics. As ideologies wane, ethical principles again come to the fore, like old rock formations revealed by erosion. As this happens the politician is forced into the role of articulating right and wrong, thinking aloud as societies face unimagined problems. As the old lodestars of right and wrong, like the majority religious institutions, continue to decline or fragment, politicians will be encouraged to fill the vacuum. They will find themselves required to act as tribunes against the encroaching rule of numbers over social life – of economics and accounts, of quantities over qualities. Their role will be to stand in favour of closeness to experience, of judgement, of ecological thinking instead of economics: as advocates of the principle that 'what truly counts cannot be counted'.[14] Their positions to this extent will become more personal, more obviously tied to the personalities they may project than in an ideological age when positions can be read off from affiliations.

From these three dimensions flows the fourth: practical pragmatism, the willingness to experiment with forms. The last generations of politicians were brought up to draw policy conclusions from ideological principles. In the future, with an accumulation of evidence about what works and about what good intentions generate unintended consequences, such as families eroded by a work culture, learning destroyed by schools, independence destroyed by dependence, one of the most important jobs of politics will be to process social learning and draw out its implications. It will no longer be either useful or credible for politicians simply to evangelize an ideology, bought second hand from philosophers: instead they will have of necessity to gather a more pragmatic, do-it-yourself agglomeration of ethical principles, practical experiences and innovative ideas, engaging in the never-ending construction, demolition and renovation of institutions.

Interestingly, it was precisely this kind of politics, a politics of constructed orders, that Hayek opposed on the grounds that it is inherently more authoritarian than the spontaneous order of markets which do not bring people into relationships of obligation. Yet the absence of such orders, and such people, would leave an intolerable gap. No society functions without some sub-groups, without relationships as well as contracts, without shared subcultures, and without enduring obligations. And societies can either adapt and evolve efficiently, learning from the experiences of others, or else be condemned to repeat old mistakes.

Underlying this principle is the idea that the old divide between individuals and collectives is no longer very relevant. Instead the defining questions are all about relationships: their degree of reciprocity, their richness and modulation, their quality and the values they embody. In societies increasingly shaped by communication, it may be inevitable that the primary unit of communication, the relationship, should become so important (and with it that underlying ethic of mutuality and equality which Habermas has done so much to develop).

For politics, the creation of a new practice and theory around a multiplicity of mutually rewarding and richly communicative relationships poses an historic challenge. It suggests a new role for the politician not fitting predefined roles but experimenting with new ones. And if such a cadre of social innovators and creative politicians does take root, working in the interstices of politics, economy and communication, their very success may indeed confirm the end of politics, for they will be part of that fragmentation of sovereignty and power that has undercut the central claims of modern politics. As harbingers of a more advanced, self-consciously creative society, they might even give meaning to Pierre Bourdieu's twist on a famous remark by Marx, when he asks us to imagine a society in which 'there are no politicians but at most people who engage in politics among other activities'. These are the people who may be best able to act politically in an antipolitical age, better than the professionals and the priests, fit for a world where the proportion of relationships that involve physical proximity is steadily declining. Politics in this sense would have come full circle, back to the human scales of the *polis*, and back to that sense of malleability which is always present in modernity but only truly meaningful closer to home than the great abstractions in which modern politics tried to make its home.

Notes

1 Rueschemeyer *et al. Capitalist Development and Democracy*, Polity, Cambridge, 1992.
2 M. Foucault, 'Governmentality', in G. Burchell *et al.* (eds), *The Foucault Effect*, Harvester, Hemel Hempstead, 1991, p. 103.
3 B. Guy Peter, *The Politics of Taxation*, Sage, London, 1992.
4 Arthur Seldon, *Capitalism*, Blackwell, Oxford, 1990.
5 J. Schumpeter, *Capitalism, Socialism and Democracy*, Harper and Row, New York, 1975, p. 265.
6 N. Luhman, *The Differentiation of Society*, Columbia University Press, New York, 1982.
7 Lutz Niethammer, 'Posthistoire', quoted in P. Anderson, *Zones of Engagement*, Verso, London, 1992.
8 Jacques Derrida, 'Violence and metaphysics: an essay on the thought of Emmanuel Levinas', in *Writing and Difference*, University of Chicago Press, Chicago, 1978, p. 138.
9 Michel Foucault, 'On the genealogy of ethics', in L. Rabinow (ed.), *A Foucault Reader*, Blackwell, Oxford, 1986, p. 343.
10 Hannah Arendt, *The Human Condition*, Chicago University Press, Chicago, 1970.
11 Alasdair MacIntyre, *After Virtue*, Duckworth, London, 1981.
12 Robert Bellah *et al.*, *Habits of the Heart*, University of California Press, Berkeley, 1985, and *The Good Society*, Alfred Knopf, New

York, 1991, are both detailed investigations of the social and institutional foundations of virtue and community.

13   Charles Perrow, *Theory and Society*, 1991, p.726.
14   William Irwin Thompson, 'Introduction', in *Gaia: a way of knowing: political implications of the new biology*, Lindisfarne Press, Great Barrington, Mass., 1987, p. 33.

2

THE PARADOX OF
EQUALITY

It is always healthy to be wary of golden ages. But to the extent that we can be certain, there are strong grounds for believing that, although man and woman are not born equal, there is an important sense in which the human race was. The great majority of the growing evidence from archaeology, palaeopathology and the various other sciences that reconstruct ancient life reveals that, before the advent of agriculture, most people lived in relatively egalitarian societies, unencumbered with food or monetary surpluses to hoard and subject only quite occasionally to bouts of warfare and genocide.

This half-submerged memory of an elysian time, before metals, farming, professional warfare and social division, has long cast its spell over religion and politics, in stories of lost golden ages and millennial returns. The difficult questions, however, concern its significance. According to one strand of argument, present since the time of the French Revolution, the single most important goal of politics has been to re-establish the equality of provision and respect of primordial humanity, albeit in a modern form. For their opponents, by contrast, growing inequality and differentiation, the extension of impersonal laws and rules, and escape from the cloying bonds of community are the very hallmarks of civilization and progress.

This essay is about the evolution of this argument, and the paradox of equality in modern societies: on the one hand, the surprising, one might say extraordinary, energy its core principles have maintained (even as a dynamic economic system generates ever greater inequalities); on the other, the gradual and probably irreversible decay of its philosophical foundations and its claim to an origin in nature.

This paradox is strikingly present in everyday politics. Despite the influence of anti-egalitarian arguments and programmes, it is hard for any observer not be struck by the continuing momentum and primordial resonance of the drive to equality. In the workplace, in the family, in the fields of representation and in society at large it has a momentum which appears to draw strength less from the intellectual strength of arguments than from fundamental dynamics in the sociology of industrial nations.[1] Worldwide, despite the setbacks and the collapse of egalitarian communism, such ideas are on the ascendant, still winning battles against traditional inequalities of class, race and gender. Perhaps the strongest evidence is that the most successful national models at the end of the century, those of Japan and South Korea, Singapore and Taiwan, are built on remarkably egalitarian foundations by contrast with the earlier models of the USA and UK.

This, the centrality of equality, is something quite new. Few societies have not had some notion of equality, whether in the form of charity and compassion for the poor and suffering, or in social arrangements, such as fiestas or charities, that hide the extent of wealth and deflect envy. And few eras have been wholly without movements for equality, such as those of Mazdak and Blossius, John Ball and Gerald Winstanley. But the modern form of arguments for equality is quite distinct. The dominant arguments for mobility, for choice and for respect, rather than for an arithmetical equality of social status, are wholly of their time. As Ernest Gellner has pointed out, the strong modern ideology of equality could emerge only when the requisite social conditions were in place: when feudal societies began to be replaced by more open, vertically and horizontally mobile ones, when national cultures replaced religious and local ones, when merit came to be the determinant of social success, when the logics of knowledge and competence came to replace birth as justifications for social status, and above all when it came to be accepted that people should be treated according to what they do rather than where they come from.

It may be, as Gellner argues, that 'Liberty, Equality and Fraternity' have turned out to be 'Bureaucracy, Mobility and Nationality',[2] but this in fact merely reinforces the point, for such a society treats all the nation's citizens without favour. More than 200 years after 1789, at the core of almost every advanced industrial society, acting both as a glue and as a motivator, is a powerful ideology concerned with fair rewards and treatment, with mobility and the eradication of barriers and irrelevant discriminations. It is an ideology devoid of any essentialist distinctions between different classes of human being, suitable for a society without any sharp social breaks. So ubiquitous is it – far more so than the ideologies of socialism, conservatism or liberalism – that all of the familiar ideologies have had to adapt around it.

Let me take just two examples. One is the commitment to equal treatment – primarily equal access to the law, equal rights in politics and equal treatment by public institutions. At first this looks like an old belief, traceable directly to the Athenian principles of isonomia, isotimia and isegoria (equality before the law, equal respect, and equal freedom of speech and political action). Yet it is probably only in this century that it has become first a majority belief, then a common sense, and subsequently something akin almost to a sacred principle for the industrial democracies, for parties of the right as much as for those on the left.

A second is opportunity. Equal opportunity (and the implication that the state must do something about it) is no longer controversial in theory (few are still interested in Michael Young's argument that it creates the smuggest elites in history), even if in practice any measure to limit the ability of one generation to pass on privileges to the next is fiercely fought (such as private schools or inheritance tax). As Christopher Jencks has written, this idea, which was once so radical, has become so denuded of content that it is now 'an ideal consistent with almost every vision of a good society'. Indeed, far from being a clarion call for radical reform, the 'constant reiteration of such rhetoric . . . may be the price we have to pay for gluing together a complex society'.[3]

It would horrify conservatives of another era that the principles of equal treatment and opportunity have extended even amid reactionary times, yet this is surely the case. Even the new right of the late twentieth century tended to couch its arguments in a populist egalitarianism, directed against the unfair accretions of power of politicians and bureaucrats, and even conservative leaders have to use a rhetoric of opportunity for all, classlessness and mobility.

They do these things because they have to. Non-egalitarian philosophies have turned out to be unsustainable in democratic societies, whereas those promising some redistribution of power and income have tended to succeed. Nor has it been lost on rulers that elites have rarely remained in power unless legitimized by an apparently neutral process that allocates reward according to merit. Perhaps most telling of all is the fact that even the attacks on egalitarian communism and redistributive social democracy used types of egalitarian argument in relation to the unfair privileges of an elite in the first case, and the unmerited rewards for the workshy or dependent poor in the second, which offend against popular notions of social justice.

Why then, if there is such a consensus in favour of practical egalitarianism, is the issue still so fraught? Why are egalitarian movements in political retreat? One answer is that egalitarian ideas remain nothing more than ideology, masks for the survival of profoundly unequal societies. Their victory has ben achieved at the expense of vacuity, which has robbed them of conviction. To some extent this is clearly the case: meritocratic ideologies, and the great privileges afforded by education, provide a wonderful legitimation for dominant classes whch remain fairly successful at reproducing themselves from generation to gneration.[4] But such a view surely underestimates the functional link between the fluidity of social structures and occupations in highly innovative societies and egalitarian ideas. If the egalitarian rhetoric were only skin-deep, you might expect a pervasive and bitter tension which is just not there.

A more obvious reason for the uncertainties of egalitarian arguments is that few agree on what is being equalized. Evidently there is wide agreement about some goods, such as political and legal rights. Yet beyond these the debate becomes confused. Should it be income and wealth that are equalized, or such things as 'liberty and opportunity, income and wealth and the bases of self-respect' (Rawls)? Should it be 'life chances' (Dahrendorf), 'choices' (Le Grand), mental and material resources (Dworkin), the capabilities to achieve 'functionings' such as participation in the community or longevity (Sen), or access to advantage (Cohen)? Or should we follow Michael Walzer in arguing for distinct approaches to equality in each of the various spheres of society to ensure that no one good (such as money, or birth) is monopolized and then used, through its terms of exchange, to dominate all other spheres? In other words, should the argument about equality be broken down into separate spheres – such as health, law, office – where different principles of distribution should reign, or should we instead insist on the links between different spheres, such as those between domestic norms and women's position in the labour market?[5]

Philosophical Roots

I suspect that the unease in all these arguments is partly philosophical: an intuitive understanding that the philosophical roots are in fact far weaker than the historical and social ones. The foundation of all of these arguments, which came to fruition in modernity, is pre-modern. Possibly drawing on that pre-agricultural heritage, the idea of equality emerged in historical times with a strong and unambiguous religious component, dating back to the Stoics in Greece (for whom all reasoning beings are equal and consequently warrant equal treatment) and early Christianity (St Augustine, for example, wrote of man in the state of innocence as equal and free). It is, after all, a cardinal principle of Christianity that in front of God all men are equal; and judged by Him according to equal criteria. There are no special favours or privileges.

It was from these theories about divine reason that the secular versions of natural law associated with Locke, Rousseau and Montesquieu developed. The great majority of modern arguments for equality can be traced back to these ideas, and to their view of humans as fundamentally equal and worthy of equal respect. All share a belief in the essential equality of man that is found when all the contingent social forms of rank and status are stripped away.

There can be no doubt that this idea played an immensely important historical role, for it provided a powerful argument against all traditional inequalities and privileges which were in this sense against nature, while also resonating with the underlying religious beliefs of the culture. It was this underlying strength which underpinned the dynamism both of the liberal case (going back to Locke and others) and of the socialist tradition (from Rousseau onwards), since both could be at one and the same time rational and religious. Indeed, it is because of the strength of this tradition of natural law that throughout the modern age, in Isaiah Berlin's words, 'the assumption is that equality needs no reasons, only inequality does so'.[6]

Where then do such natural law arguments stand today? The answer is surely that their work has now been done. We are much further from a shared religious culture than was the case 200 years ago. Few societies retain the homogeneity and certainty of belief which is implicitly assumed by arguments from nature. Nowadays we judge people not by their relation to God, but rather by their relations to other people and to social institutions. We draw our lessons from experience and knowledge rather than from first principles, and we are brought up to doubt the value of cognitive validations of social realities. The result is that natural law and state of nature arguments seem out of kilter with everything we know about the world. They cannot help but sound archaic, even when couched in the apparently modern language of rights.

If they are not prepared to make leaps of faith, people now want stronger reasons to believe in anything, and they want evidence. Even in this highly contested field this is far from impossible, since there is a considerable body of empirical evidence about equality. The merits of positive discrimination programmes, for example, can be judged by evidence about their costs (in resentment and self-doubt) and their benefits (in substantially changing occupational patterns). The economic merits of inequality can be judged by looking at the scanty evidence that high marginal tax rates encourage people to work less, the stronger evidence that they encourage evasion, and the more circumstantial evidence that they erode the cultural foundations of risk and enterprise. Looking at societies as a whole, there is probably some significance in the correlations between income equality and growth or longevity, even if one should be very cautious about ascribing causation.[7] Such studies of the objective facts of equality can also be linked to a considerable body of work on popular attitudes to equality and social justice, which tend to bring out the gap between the public view that rewards should be linked to effort and desert and the philosophers' more abstract rules of distribution (Nozick and Rawls, for example, have almost nothing to say about desert).[8]

For those seeking reasons for holding views about equality, there is also the knowledge to be drawn from personal experience and the experience passed down by culture, which confirms that privilege or background do not make people inherently better, that different people have very different strengths and that these are rarely immediately visible or apparent, and that almost everyone has a capacity for autonomy. Similarly, arguments from fields like genetics can show that differences within 'races' are far greater than differences between races,[9] while educational theorists can demonstrate the variety of types of intelligence which belie crude estimations of people's worth.[10]

It should be evident that arguments of this kind are all more pertinent today to a modern politics than Locke or Aquinas. But it should also be clear that they are much weaker types of argument, and at most not arguments for absolute equality, but rather arguments that if people are to be treated differently than there have to be clear and convincing arguments why this should be the case.

The Historical Origins of Opposition to Inequality

If the philosophical foundations are cracked, and possibly less significant than prosaic sources of knowledge, what is the foundation for an egalitarian perspective that can be shared by people from different religious and cultural backgrounds? In some respects the answer may be the same as in the past. Equality may be less important as an idea in itself than as an offshoot of universal human emotions of compassion, emotions which are at best constrained in poor societies, but which come to the fore in more prosperous and stable ones. It is intuitively convincing that the various movements for greater equality have drawn their greatest strength not from widespread support for arithmetical equality or sameness, but rather from an anger against lack and deprivation. The anger stems from the poverty of the poor more than the wealth of the rich; wealth is only morally repugnant when set against a backcloth of unmet need.

Historically, too, it is probably fair to say that the case for equality has been based less on any desire for pure equality than on the common concern of wealthy altruists and a poor majority to overcome the likely implications of inequality: denial of the basic means of life such as food, security, homes, health and fuel; denial of the means of realizing the full potentials of life, on the grounds of some moral idea of what humans are for, and of what consciousness can achieve; and the domination and oppression which result from unequal access to social goods, and which obviously undermine autonomy.

These consequences obviously cover quite a wide gamut. But the central one, and the one that has provided most of the rhetoric for equality, is material deprivation. Here the argument taps into something universal: the charity and concern which can be found in cultures throughout history and in all regions. All that changes is that in modern society the state becomes the vehicle for charity rather than the church, or the face-to-face encounter of supplicant and giver.

However, there is an important respect in which this type of argument is circumscribed. The compassionate desire to ensure that all have the basic material conditions of life is very different from compassion that could persuade people to act to eliminate relative inequality. Compassion depends on the fact that everyone has the same basic material needs for food, warmth, shelter and security. That is why we can literally (and this is the root of the word 'compassion') 'feel with' other people. This too is probably why there is such a strong intuitive understanding that health care should be provided equally according to need: in the face of death and disease we are all equal and able to empathize with each other. Beyond these common needs, however, our needs become much more differentiated, and thus less susceptible to empathy and compassion. It is much harder to feel compassion for someone denied the means to go to a karate class, to see their nation triumph at war or to have a really good foreign holdiay. Compassion probably works only at the lower end of the famous hierarchy of needs devised by Abraham Maslow, which starts from common basic needs at the bottom, and rises through stages to reach the more complex ones, such as psychic needs for self-realization, where there is an infinity of variety.

The political implication of this is obvious. To the extent that egalitarian arguments base themselves on a moral opposition to poverty and material deprivation, on compassion and altruism, they have to accept fairly tight limits. They work only as arguments for eliminating absolute rather than relative poverty. Indeed, in a world of continuing starvation, they fall apart if used within a national community to justify redistribution from a wealthy elite to a materially secure, but relatively poor subordinate group.

This is surely why egalitarian arguments seem to bifurcate in most modern societies. Whereas in traditional and early modern societies, the majority has a clear material interest in redistributing wealth from a privileged minority, this ceases to be the case in mature industrial societies. As basic material deprivations are largely solved, and as the social structure is transformed from the pyramid of premodern society into the modern oblong, the issues of equality divide into two.

One set of issues concerns equality in the interests of the majority. In all modern societies, the distribution of access to human capital and job opportunities, which are the key determinants of social position, tends to remain both unequal and subject to discriminations (such as by gender) that cannot be rationally justified. The result is a strong practical interest in reform, since even though removal of a particular discrimination may not be in the interests of the majority (for example, discrimination according to race), the general principle of equal and non-discriminatory treatment is clearly in the majority interest. For reasons already given, this majority interest also seems to go with the grain of the functional needs of a modern society for flexibility and adaptability, and a transparent and legitimate distribution of rewards.

The second set of issues concern the often substantial proportion of the population which continues to be cut off from opportunities and rewards, and which remains subject to material deprivation (including new deprivations which arise from growth, such as the need for a car which results from suburbanization or declining public transport).[11] Whereas the first set of issues are about a sharing of dynamic opportunities, this second debate tends to be more about what economics calls comparative statics, one-off redistributions of income: as Arthur Okun put it, secondary, politically justified distributions of rewards superimposed on the market. We have already seen why the limits of compassion make such redistributions harder to justify than moves to equal treatment and equal opportunity. But there is also another, perhaps deeper reason.

The idea of equality of result, with its origins in religion and natural law, conflicts directly with the core industrial ideas of mobility and merit that sustain the principles of equal treatment and opportunity. Given differential ability and work, equal results appear unfair (and even Marx only moves from 'each according to his ability' to 'each according to his needs' once there is abundance). Albert Hirschman has also suggested another, parallel reason why the idea of equal result has always been difficult to sell politically. He suggests that contentment depends not only on people's level of rewards, but also on two other things: on the expectation of future rewards, and on the sense of fairness of reward relative to others.[12] He correctly contrasts the 'comparative statics' of much egalitarian argument to the dynamic contexts in which they actually have to be justified. Thus his argument explains why, in increasingly unequal conditions, social cohesion is often possible if enough people are confident that their rewards will improve in the future, or if the culture is successful in persuading them that their meagre reward reflects their meagre contribution. His argument also confirms that equality of result will win support only if it is seen to be fair, and if the prevailing culture, forms of life and structures of communication make people particularly aware of the needs of others and thus of why an equal distribution may be fair. Without such intensive communication (and a strong community) it is hard to see how a distribution which does not accord with the higher ideals of the society (which as we have seen are primarily concerned with merit and opportunity, hard work and responsibility) will be legitimate.

Clearly, this argument undermines any pure egalitarianism which seems 'obviously' unfair (even if responsibility and hard and dirty work are also distributed equally). But it also interestingly shows some of the limits of pure free market arguments which claim that the market determines rewards justly through the interaction of demand and supply, the marginal utility of consumers and the willingness to work. It remains the case that few accept the absolute fairness of such a distribution, which may have only a partial relationship to merit and hard work, particularly when societies with large public sectors are continually having to make public appraisals of the relative worth of professors and teachers, orderlies and postal workers, thus politicizing the whole question of reward. Indeed, it is significant that the pure liberal free marketeer has to resort to a species of natural law argument to avoid this problem: all people, so it is claimed, are equal before the market (which takes over from God), whereas the social and political distribution of reward is intrinsically vulnerable to unwarranted discrimination.[13]

The Elimination of Poverty

If these are the very real limits to arguments for equality of result, how is the elimination of poverty justified other than through arguments for compassion? I want to argue that three types of argument remain, each in a different way making an appeal to majority interest.

The first is the now familiar argument for social cohesion. Excess inequality and poverty, so it is argued, cause social disorder, conflict and high rates of crime which erode the quality of life of the majority, and which more subtly undermine the moral foundations of a society. Furthermore, whereas in a traditional society considerable inequalities could be legitimate, and compatible with social cohesion, in a modern society which continually promises mobility and opportunity, those at the bottom of the social hierarchy are less likely to accept their position and more likely to react either through political rebellion or through seeking self-validation in crime. Consequently, it is in the interests of the majority to eliminate socially divisive inequalities.

Such an argument is, of course, much stronger where there is a real sense of community. With shared media and culture, a density of communications and friendships and interactions across social boundaries, the costs of social fragmentation are much more evident than in atomized societies locked into top-down media. Such an argument also requires acceptance that there is an economic background to the boredom, the dearth of excitement and meaning, which are primary causes of much crime. Nevertheless even in the most fragmented society these arguments have some purchase, simply because it is practically difficult to achieve a full insulation from the material and psychic condition of others. Where this is bad, and where there is resentment either against the successful or against the society as a whole, the quality of life of the better-off tends to diminish, vulnerable to what Edward Luttwak, in an American context, has described as 'internal intifadas'.[14]

The second argument derives from the idea of human potential and claims that there is a common interest, whether of the locality, the nation or even of the species as a whole, in realizing to the full people's potential qualities, whether as inventors, entrepreneurs, carers or healers. Because of the complex nature of human qualities (one thinks, for example, of Howard Gardner's seven types of human intelligence)[15] it is likely that most existing systems for determining merit will miss important qualities, and that there is therefore a common interest in supporting generous frameworks for eliminating any inequalities which act to block individuals' ability to realize their talents. This argument can be made either in an economic language of human capital and national competitiveness or more broadly: at the limit, the interest of the species as a whole in using all its resources to ensure that it survives.

Interestingly, it is an argument that recalls Marx, who was never a simple advocate of equality. The whole structure of Marx's case was built around the concept of the all-round developed individual as the goal of human history. This is not to be achieved through rights and natural law arguments, since equal rights are 'a right of inequality like every right'. Rather the 'free development of each as the condition of the free development of all' is to be achieved through the inner logic of history, resolving any apparent contradiction between freedom and equality on the higher plane of material abundance and genuine autonomy.

Such an argument, which resonates with much of libertarian thought, raises the old question of the link between inequality and domination. One of the strongest arguments against any inequality is that it entails a relationship of domination which diminishes the person being dominated. Many would go further and wish to be able to choose to live in a society which had reduced domination, and advanced beyond the authoritarian and servile characters which relations of domination bring. This is an inherently pleasing idea. But, as Michael Walzer shows, it is not of itself a very useful principle, for it depends crucially on how inequality and domination are to be reduced. If, for example, the state takes responsibility for distributing power equally, then in practice state power simply replaces money as the key social good, the one social good which can be exchanged for all others, and, as such, is just as likely to be used to constrain autonomy.[16] In other words, politics on its own cannot solve problems of domination and inequality, although it certainly can assist: those who wish to live in a society free from domination, and in which the free development of each is bound up with the free development of all, need to be concerned with all the spheres of society and not just with the relation between the state and money. To put the argument another way, in a world which as yet has no experience of societies without power, autonomy is best served not by the elimination of domination, but rather by bringing an end to unjustifiable and unremovable power.

Both the arguments described above, the argument for social cohesion and the argument for potential and autonomy, can be made to people at all levels in a society. They are directed neither solely at the self-interest of the direct beneficiaries of any redistribution, nor solely at the altruistic benevolence of the privileged. Moreover, both can be made either in an ethical form, highlighting the moral unacceptability of social conflict or human waste, or in a practical way, explaining why investment in the well-being of others, their education or housing, can have indirect material benefits for those doing the paying.

What then are their flaws, and why is their merit not self-evident? Much of the political scepticism has arisen because of a broader doubt about the capacities of government. But there are also causes to be found in the history of disappointments of the war against poverty, which have meant that arguments for action to reduce inequality have repeatedly stepped back from their earlier positions. One hundred years ago it was believed, self-evidently, that poverty was a problem of money. If money was redistributed through pensions and unemployment benefit, social security and public services, decent public housing and employment creation, inequality would diminish and poverty would disappear. To some extent this analysis was and remains correct: those countries with well-run and generous welfare provision drastically cut poverty (and such benefits are far more important than taxes).[17] Transfers do diminish inequality in countries like Germany and the Netherlands, unlike Australia and Canada. Sweden's system, for example, removes nearly four times as many people from poverty as the USA, particularly because of its treatment of pensions.

But simple transfers are by their nature ameliorative rather than being solutions. They are downstream rather than upstream policies. As a result, the argument stepped back from the surface evidence of income inequalities to their apparent causes. Unless the means of achieving status and position were redistributed, little would change. Since education was correctly recognized as the decisive creator of opportunity and the key social marker, the big anti-poverty programmes, such as Lyndon Johnson's Great Society initiatives, put considerable effort into directing educational opportunities to the poor. By redistributing the means for people to participate fully in the economy and society, the need for perpetual income redistribution would disappear.

Symbolic Deprivation

To some extent these programmes were effective, certainly in providing good opportunities for a minority, although the realities of political power meant that more resources were almost always put into provision for middle-class areas, particularly in the USA. But even if this had not been the case, it became clear that education alone would achieve little, and that one step behind the apparent opportunities of an open, merit-based society lay entrenched cultural differences that contribute to motivation, to self-esteem and to people's sense of their own possibilities. As a result, the debate moved on yet again, to look at role-models and leadership, to the cultivation of self-esteem, and to the importance of cultures that legitimate subordinate groups. The more poverty has been analysed, the more it has become clear just how important are those subtle social dividers such as family structure and culture, and the more it has become clear that the old comment that if you took away all the wealth of the top 5 per cent they would be back on top within a generation remains relevant. Indeed, where there is a degree of 'symbolic deprivation', a lack of self-esteem and a lack of validation in the dominant culture, redistributive measures may simply exacerbate inequality. Welfare dependence and, to a lesser extent, measures of positive discrimination, simply become markers of subordination and sources of stigma.

These comments confirm what every anthropologist assumes, namely that symbolic inequalities are as significant as material ones. But it is only fairly recently that this has been shown in detail in relation to advanced societies. The work of Pierre Bourdieu, for example, has shown with intricate care how in modern societies class and power operate along at least two dimensions – economic capital, and cultural or symbolic capital – and how the educational system works as an ingenious legitimator of inequalities which are reproduced from generation to generation.[18] His schema explains why the culturally inept self-made businessman is in many ways less powerful than the relatively poor novelist, university lecturer or teacher, and why so many of the decisive battles in modern societies take place around the terms of exchange between cultural and economic capital: entrepreneurs trying to denounce professors and artists, and vice versa, popular newspapers attacking the idle chattering intellectuals, and the latter attacking barbarous materialism in return.

The political problem, if one accepts the validity of arguments for social cohesion and individual potential, is therefore acute. Does one fatalistically accept human society's ability to resist any attempt to impose equality? Or does one distinguish those elements of self-esteem which work as a zero-sum game (more assertive women necessarily implying more insecure men, a more self-confident black culture necessarily bringing forth a resentful racist reaction), and those which work in a positive-sum game (since on the face of it a society of high-esteem individuals and subgroups should also have greater collective self-confidence and economic welfare)? Does it become a social imperative to distinguish those goods, described by Fred Hirsch as positional,[19] whose scarcity no amount of prosperity can diminish, such as country homes, honours or fame, and those sources of psychic reward which can be multiplied more easily?

The earlier arguments would suggest that these questions are worth answering, and that there is scope for positive-sum games, even if these are likely to be much more difficult to achieve than the old mechanistic understandings of redistribution would have assumed. There are, after all, many different ways to organize a society, some more cohesive and productive than others, and in the conditions of reflexive modernity, when knowledge about societies feeds back into their modes of organization, there are no immutable status quos and natural orders.

These arguments therefore have two implications. The first is that the political justification for action on poverty will be much stronger if it goes beyond altruism and into the various types of 'majority interest' argument set out above. The second is that any such action must be effective if it is to remain legitimate, which in turn depends on simultaneously addressing three distinct levels: the material conditions of housing, food, fuel and security; the components of human capital (and how these become practically accessible to the single mother or the inner-city teenager); and the culture, above all the lack of self-esteem, which provides the context for poverty.

Equality Beyond Morality

For all its modernity, it remains quite possible that the belief in equality is rooted somewhere so deep in our collective memory or even in our genes that it is impossible to stand aside and judge it objectively. We may still be clinging to a lost paradise in neolithic human history when there was relative equality and relative sharing of goods and work, before material inequality, class stratification and domination came to divide the community. We may still be trying to cope with a genetic predisposition to treat others with equal respect.

But even if there is some natural or biological basis for equality, it does not follow that equality can be justified by state of nature type arguments, or by the rights type arguments that flow from them. As Alasdair MacIntyre wrote, the best reason for believing that there are no natural rights is 'of precisely the same type as the best reason which we possess for asserting that there are no witches', namely that 'every attempt . . . has failed'.[20] In a modern rational society, brought up to challenge and to doubt, no sustainable sense of equality can be derived from natural law or a priori theories (whether Locke or Rawls), and nor can any abstract grounding be found for people to support the equality of others. They can offer very powerful tools of rhetoric, and grounds for assertion and self-worth, but nothing resembling a compelling argument. The old religious roots of egalitarianism, about equality of both result and treatment, are simply less persuasive today.

But to accept this does not concede the ground of equality to those who argue against any attempt to determine collective redistributions on grounds either of justice or of practicality. Nor does it extract the ethics from highly moral issues. Instead it does quite the opposite. By situating the issue of equality within its true historical context, and by making practical arguments which strip away the obfuscation of so much thinking about equality, the issues actually become clearer. Results can be stripped away from intentions, faith separated from rational conclusions. Moral judgements can be brought closer to popular understandings of justice and fairness, with their often tougher ideas of desert. By accepting the fact that we live in a world that no longer shares a homogeneous religious and ethical tradition, we recognize instead that all arguments, whether ethical or otherwise, make sense only if they can make some reference to experience and learning, to the state of public attitudes and values, and to which types of society work and which do not. Morality, in other words, has come down from heaven. It is in among us, justifiable by tangible benefits and common interests, and made meaningful by the lived experience of communities, or else it is nowhere.

Notes

1 Ernest Gellner, *Nations and Nationalism*, Blackwell, Oxford, 1983.
2 E. Gellner, *Plough, Sword and Book*, Palladin, London, 1991.
3 C. Jencks, in N. Bowie (ed.) *Equal Opportunity*, Westview, London, 1978.
4 This is the argument, for example, of much of Pierre Bourdieu's work, from 'Reproduction', in *Education, Society and Culture* (with J.-C. Passeron), Sage, London, 1977.

5   M. Okin, *Justice, Gender and the Family*, Basic Books, New York, 1989.
6   I. Berlin, 'Equality', in F. Olagson (ed.), *Justice and Social Policy*, Prentice Hall, London, 1961, p. 131.
7   See, for example, Richard Douthwaite, *The Growth Illusion*, Green Books, Bideford, 1992.
8   See, for example, J. Kluegel and E. Smith, *Beliefs about Inequality*, Aldine de Gruyter, New York, 1986, and M. Deutsch, *Distributive Justice*, Yale University Press, New Haven, 1985.
9   Steve Jones, The BBC Reith Lectures, 1991.
10 Howard Gardner, *Frames of Mind*, Harvard University Press, Cambridge, Mass., 1983.
11 C. Jencks, *Inequality*, Allen Lane, London, 1973.
12 Albert Hirschman, 'The changing tolerance of income inequality', in *Essays in Trespassing* Cambridge University Press, Cambridge, 1981.
13 See, for example, Arthur Seldon, *Capitalism*, Blackwell, Oxford, 1990.
14 Edward Luttwak, *Times Literary Supplement*, 22 May 1992, p. 9.
15 Howard Gardner, *Frames of Mind*, op. cit.
16 Michael Walzer, *Spheres of Justice*, Basic Books, New York, 1983.
17 J. Pechman, *Tax, Reform: the rich and the poor*, Harvester Wheatsheaf, London, 1989.
18 P. Bourdieu, *Distinction*, Routledge, London, 1989.
19 Fred Hirsch, *The Social Limits to Growth*, Routledge, London, 1977.
20 Alasdair MacIntyre, *After Virtue*, Duckworth, London, 1981.

3

CITIZENS AND
RESPONSIBILITIES

The debate about citizenship stretches back over 2000 years and beyond to the ancient republics of Greece and Rome. But the renewed interest of the late twentieth century reflects the special concerns of our times. Today's arguments about citizenship derive their conviction from a dissatisfaction with everything from the state of the environment to the standards of public life. They are inevitably touched by the general disillusion with politics and by fears about the decay of civic values and social solidarity. Citizenship appears as a prism through which a happier order can be imagined. Indeed, at times the word becomes so devoid of meaning that almost any idea can cast itself in the language of citizenship. Yet there is, for all that, a common metatheme, lying behind these other concerns and giving them a hard edge. It is a theme without which claims about citizenship must always remain incomplete. At its core is the idea of responsibility.

After lying dormant for decades, responsibility has again become popular in political discourse. It is being invoked by politicians and religious and civic leaders throughout the world, as a necessary part of any solutions to the state of the environment, of inequality or of urban life. In the rhetoric of corporate responsibility it is being used, sometimes cynically, by businesses eager to show their commitment to community. In Rene Dubos' influential slogan 'think globally, act locally' there is an implicit affirmation of the link between social responsibility and individual action. And in much of the thinking about the long-term impact of paternalistic welfare states there has been an intense concern with how responsibility can be fostered among individuals, families and institutions.

These arguments about responsibility have proved resistant to any easy appropriation. They are neither obviously right wing nor left wing. They challenge both the unfairness and amorality of the market and the diffusion of responsibility brought about by industrial socialism. They suggest that the world's deficits of responsibility can be solved only by a new ethos for individuals and a new affirmation of what it means to live as part of a community. And if the left's recent concern has been to reconcile equality with freedom, these arguments suggest that neither makes much sense unless grounded in an ethos of mutual responsibility.

This essay suggests some of the ways in which responsibility might be taken more seriously. It argues that the left's thinking on freedom and power has often been unbalanced because of a failure to address problems of responsibility. It suggests that individual responsibility brings out the best in people, and that communities work better if they are rooted in shared responsibilities. It argues that any society which loses the capacity to hold people responsible and to use the power of blame and shame will pay a heavy price. And it concludes that the only coherent ideological alternatives to the unfettered market are those that make links between individual responsibility and what the community can do to help people take control over their lives.

Across the world three historic moments have forced these issues on to the political agenda. The first has been the collapse of communism. A large part of its failure was practical, an inability to make things work. But equally important was its failure to be responsible, either in the sense of being accountable to those on the receiving end of decisions or in the sense of having an ethos of responsible behaviour. Instead power corrupted and absolute power corrupted absolutely. Marxism-Leninism offered no guidance as to how individuals should use power, and no standards of truth and propriety.

As a result, many of the most magnetic ideas in the East today come from those who assert the obligation of the individual and community to truth and responsibility. Vaclav Havel, Sakharov and Fang Lizhi have all invoked high standards of personal behaviour as a starting point for any credible politics. All have denounced the impact of a totalitarian, corrupted and amoral society in corroding any sense of individual responsibility.

The second moment has been the environmental crisis. The green movement calls to account the responsibility not only of politicians and industrialists but also of the human species. For the deep greens, humans bear responsibilities to other species and to life itself. Some argue for a wholesale retreat from super-industrial civilization on the grounds that only then can human power be brought into line with humans' capacity to use it responsibly.

In its more political forms the green movement has successfully called for regulations and taxes to make the polluter pay, for a more responsible ethos of consumption, and for the political system to impose responsibility on to those who cause damage. One of the great appeals of green ideas is their claim that the individual can act in practical, everyday ways to achieve change, rather than waiting for states to find collective solutions.

A third moment arises from the evident crisis of the new right. Responsibility was always an important element in neoconservative rhetoric. A strong emphasis on personal responsibility justified moves to reduce people's dependence on the state. Margaret Thatcher's proud boast of her first administration was that it had achieved a shift away from a state which was 'totally dominant in people's lives and penetrated almost every aspect of life to a life where the state did do certain things, but without displacing personal responsibility'.

Under this philosophy everything from workfare type training schemes (designed to eliminate dependence), through the restructured social fund (teaching the responsible use of welfare money) to the opting out of schools and council house sales could be justified. Thatcherism promised a massive passing out of responsibility from the state to families and individuals. An argument about responsibility was also used in relation to government.

The neoconservatives promised to make the government which survived their treatment into a responsible creature, not spending more than it could legitimately earn. That 'spare and stingy creature' in the words of Ronald Reagan's infamous budget director, David Stockman, would abide by the rules of good housekeeping. Adherence to strict monetary targets and the elimination of public borowing were designed to block what people like Milton Friedman saw as the inherent irresponsibility and upward bidding of democratic politics.

Responsibility underpinned the moral virtue of the right. The left could be characterized as spending without earning, as creating dependency and sapping the self-responsibility of people and communities. It could be shown as engaged in a perpetual search for alibis, blaming every ill on society or others. Under socialism the buck would never stop.

Property rights provided the means for creating a responsible society. The public sector would literally be sold in parcels, public goods turned into private ones. Part of the rationale was that the property owner would be responsible and take the long view, conserving and husbanding resources. By contrast, the individual who shares a tiny part of a collectively owned good has little immediate incentive to value it. According to the theory, property inculcates care, collectivism carelessness.

So much for the ideas. The practice has been somewhat different. The Reagan and Thatcher years turned out to be extraordinarily irresponsible times. Far from government behaving responsibly, American public deficits soared. Selfishness and greed, and corruption in government and business, came to be the hallmarks of the neoconservative era. In the USA at least, a populist backlash emerged which gathered momentum with the election of President Clinton.

The practical failures of classic monetarism, Laffer curves and underresearched welfare reforms were amplified by the right's failure to resolve the tension btween conservatism and libertarianism. It has found no stable balance between the maximization of freedom and a strong ethos of responsibility, or, for that matter, between liberation and social order. The theoreticians may be satisfied by the trick of dissolving responsibility into its abstractions, the market and freedom, but the public will always remain unconvinced if at the same time it faces rising crime rates and a crescendo of financial corruption.

The same tension compromises the market. It is true that anyone living by the laws of the market has to earn what they spend (within admittedly broad limits), to plan and to care for their assets. But equally, all markets bring very strong incentives to evade responsibilities: to pass costs on to the community and to devalue the future and what is left to later generations. Property rights foster care within narrow limits but only at the price of carelessness in relation to the rest of society. Moreover, the market's moral persuasiveness is corroded when almost any action can be jusified as a response to 'market discipline' and when almost any provider of an amoral product or service can claim that the real fault lies with the demands of the general public.

The faultlines in right-wing ideology run deep. Responsibility is both etymologically and philosophically a social concept. It means literally 'answerability'. It is an idea born of the assumption that people live in communities and that they answer to each other. It is, as a result, ill at ease in any political theory that starts with the atomized individual, and assumes that people are only greedy, grasping and competitive. This is why attempts to reroot the right through concepts such as active citizenship have proven difficult. If the philosophical base is individualism, and an individualism that is predisposed to selfish, greedy action, then it is hard to explain why anyone should behave responsibly except under coercion.

For the left, the right's failure to articulate a credible vision of a responsible society should open opportunities. The right is again vulnerable to the charge that it is immoral, presiding over falling standards in everything from environment and education to public life, an explosion of personal debt and a squandering of resources. But it would be wrong to conclude that the left can push at an open door. For the arguments about responsibility suggest that socialized forms can dissipate responsibility as much as the market. They throw the problem back on to the individual. They emphasize ethos and morality over structure and interest, universal values over political economy. And although they recognize the role of the state in providing people with the conditions to live and realize themselves, they also appreciate the dangers of letting the state monopolize responsibility.

This is unfamiliar terrain for much of the left. Questions of responsibility have been underplayed for many years, reflecting socialist thought's movement away from its Christian roots towards politics with a capital 'P' and a concern with structure. The shift is all too apparent in today's fashionable codewords, which are all about the decentralization of power. The words 'enabling', 'empowerment', 'citizenship' and 'consumerism' are all about dispersing power. The state is to be broken down and distributed fairly, for the right by granting people entitlement in the market, for the left by giving them powers through local democratic institutions or constitutionally guaranteed rights. Some take the concepts further, arguing for action to distribute the competences people need in order to use power or rights effectively. But the general point is widely shared and has rapidly taken hold as a new common sense.

While the right has learnt the power of libertarian radical democratic and populist arguments, the left the organizational virtues of markets, both have lost something. Both have become embarrassed by moral arguments. Both have come to see power as a commodity that can be distributed and parcelled up, the state as a body that can choose to give this or that section of the population units of empowerment. Once received, power is simply there to be used. A Santa Claus state dishes out powers without making demands on those receiving them. Left and right compete as to the attractiveness of what is to be distributed. The right offers tax cuts, subsidized council houses and utility shares, the left regional assemblies and citizens' rights, training credits and denominational schools.

For parties and states to be engaged in a competition to wither away is certainly novel historically and not without its attractions. But it leaves difficult questions unanswered. One is that, to be meaningful, decentralization must entail a distribution of responsibility as well as power. This implies that there will be failures and that some will pay a price for their inability to use power effectively. It implies that empowered citizens must also be prepared to face the full weight of punishment for antisocial actions. It directly challenges the libertarians, who oppose any idea that citizenship entails any obligations: where, after all, does such an accretion of rights end? It justifies unease about a fragmented, heterogeneous postmodern world where there are no universal solidarities and mutual responsibilities.

I shall come back to these questions later. At this stage it is enough to recognize that decentralization can free those with power from the responsibility to use it well, and offer politicians a perfect alibi. Having privatized and decentralized, they can simply shrug their shoulders and say 'none of my business' when disasters happen. The same incentives apply to the machinery of government. The new right used to argue that the classic impulse of both politicians and bureaucrats was to build empires. Yet throughout the 1980s and 1990s states of all political stripes happily divested themselves of functions. The reason is simple. Like the modern corporation, the most rational and perceptive modern bureaucracy aims to maximize its power and minimize its responsibilities. To do this it slims itself down to a strategic core and hives off all operational functions. While maintaining strategic control and all the perks of power, it can justly claim innocence when anything goes wrong.

Freedom and Licence

While throwing off its identification with the overbearing state, the left has been desperate to identify with freedom. Left, right and centre justify their actions as expanding the realm of freedom. It is the one unquestioned ideal, with almost no visible enemies outside of Beijing, Baghdad and a few other forsaken places.

This is in almost every way a good thing. To anyone living under tyranny there is nothing more important than freedom. It is a pressing, almost palpable need. It is the necessary condition for life itself. But 'come the revolution' it turns out that, while freedom may have been a necessary condition, it is sufficient for nothing. It does not give any clues as to how to behave to others; how to share; how to think; or how to feel. It tells us nothing about judgement, about right or wrong. It simply refers from the social to the individual all the big problems. At its worst, the rhetoric of freedom represents the conquest of meaning by vacuity.

This is as true of the Marxist left as of the libertarian right. Marxism has been notoriously silent on the problems of power. While much of its intellectual labour went into detailing the manifold forms of power, economic, ideological, cultural, it was easy to succumb to the utopian belief that in the future power could be eliminated and replaced by freedom without compromise. If the end is a society without power and without states and mediated representatives, there are no problems of responsibility and accountability. It is a characteristic of modern utopias that they maximize freedom. They never maximize responsibilities, though it is arguable that the bearing of responsibility is as much an end of human potential as the exercise of freedom. In this sense, utopias are childlike. Like the worst demagogues, they promise without demanding.

In the past there was a clear distinction between freedom and licence, between freedom and freedom to do the right thing. This distinction between choice and the individual's duty to use it to the best is largely absent from modern political discourse. In the absence of a strong sense of right conduct, freedom has become synonymous with licence.

Accountability

The one realm where the left has consistently spoken a language of responsibility is around accountability. This idea has a long history that parallels the equation of radicalism with opposition to arbitrary power. The democratic and later the socialist revolution promised to bring power into line with responsibility and accountability. Instead of the caprice of kings and the indifference of bankers, public actions would be open to scrutiny and judgement. Anyone exercising power would have to stand or fall by their record. Government would become accountable, transparent, responsive and responsible. Those on the receiving end of power would have a chance to know what was done in their name.

There are still strong echoes of this tradition today, and much still to be achieved. Freedom of Information Acts, co-determination in companies, and democratic accountability in local affairs, in education and in public services can all be counterposed to the accretion of invisible and irresponsible power by national governments and transnational companies and organizations. This is all to the good, especially in such opaque societies as Britain. It remains true that there are too few lines of accountability, whether within firms, between service providers and users, or between planners and planned.

The problems arise when answerability works in more than one direction. We would all agree that the powerful should be answerable to the powerless. But should the powerless be answerable to each other when their actions impinge – when they pollute, when they take each other's jobs, or when they choose a distinct lifestyle? Should the individual be accountable to the community or the state? What is the employee's responsibility to the employer, the citizen's to the state? Does the young person have any obligations to the society that provides food, shelter and education? These are all new ways of posing the old question of the social contract, of whether the contract entails obligations, or whether the citizenship it describes is just another contingent relationship.

Linking Power and Responsibility

To answer these questions we have to start by recognizing that responsibility means more than just autonomy and accountability. In everyday use it also refers to something moral, to duty and obligation. Its implicit ideal, you could say, is self-regulation and self-control. This makes it unusually difficult to discuss. There is now no single moral code, no one moral high ground in any modern society. It might be more accurate to talk of many high grounds, a range of hills rather than a dominating peak.

The political challenge is not to recreate a monolithic (and, of course, usually hypocritical) past of moral homogeneity. It is rather to foster higher standards of behaviour within diversity, to create feedback loops that reward the good over the bad, and consciously to challenge that diffusion of responsibility which is a predictable and pernicious effect of increasing scale and complexity, where it is rarely easy to define lines of causality and guilt.

This means going against many of the accepted ways of doing things in the modern world. One is more than a century's faith in insurance: the idea that mistakes and misfortunes can be planned against and bought out of. This, after all, contributed to the welfare state, born in social insurance, a protective mantle from cradle to grave, while in the free market it has become possible to be insured against anything from damages claims to libel, so that under the sway of the actuarial table responsibility is replaced with probability.

A Responsible Society

It is not hard to imagine a society that took responsibility as seriously as it took freedom and equality. Some of its elements would be fairly familiar: criminals required to compensate victims (and punishments which are better suited to the nature of the crime); polluters required to clear up the mess they make; drug companies responsible for the side-effects they cause; mutual obligations between landlords and tenants; trade unions liable for the cost of disputes. Others might be less familiar: governments could promote the material and culture competences needed for responsible behaviour; investors could be held legally more accountable for the actions of those they invest in; companies could become more responsible for the livelihood of those who work for them; remuneration could be linked more to direct responsibility than to qualifications or market demands, so that the nurse and the manager would be paid more than the broker and the journalist; neighbourhoods could be required to organize their own street cleaning, policing and planning procedures, with options to opt out. Such principles of responsible behaviour could apply in all fields: heavy taxes could discourage holders of capital from skipping from industry to industry, always looking for the effortless exit; managers of council departments could become directly liable for failure to deliver a service; education could foster mutual obligation, as in the Japanese practice of group assessment. The possibilities are endless.

But any such programme immediately runs into the age-old tension between freedom and equality. Granting neighbourhoods the responsibility for managing their own litter collection, or granting regions autonomy over economic decision making, could rapidly lead to heightened inequalities. These could in turn become a source of social antagonsim and resentment against a philosophy that removes the alibis that most people seem to need in order to survive in a complex world. But rather than seeing freedom and equality as quantities to be traded off, through the prism of responsibility it is clear that they can be partially resolved. The idea of responsibility resolves the tension at a higher plane, invoking the social responsibility to pick up the needs of others. Ultimately, freedom and equality can only be resolved in a highly moral society where the strength of community makes the conflict between them meaningless.

For the radical these arguments are initially unsettling. Requiring those without the means to exercise responsibility appears deeply reactionary. It seems to favour the powerful, to provide a new set of legitimations for their power. Yet in practice it is precisely the most powerful institutions which are most immune to responsibility. Government itself is the clearest example. Apart from the blunt instrument of quinquennial elections it is very hard truly to call it to account. Legally, its sovereignty is absolute, tempered only at the edges by judicial review and complaints procedures. Companies are an equally important example. Since the invention of limited liability the licensed irresponsibility of the capitalist enterprise has been beyond question. There is only one real relationship which involves responsibility, and that is the relationship of directors and shareholders. All others, whether workers, consumers or those polluted or inconvenienced are simply bystanders. The trade unions, too, quickly learned the nature of the game and won themselves a series of legal immunities, while the professions regulate themselves precisely to limit the danger of being held responsible by the outside world.

Any serious programme for spreading responsibility would have to start not with those at the bottom of society, those out of work and on welfare, but rather with the most powerful. But its radicalism would apply across the board, for a society that was committed to devolving power as well as responsibility also entails letting people make their own disasters. In the economic sphere, 'empowerment' necessarily involves an acceptance that there will be failures and that these must hurt. Indeed, there is no escaping the implication that there must be some accountability to those whose resources are used and those whose lives are affected, whether through the courts, the self-regulating ethos of professions, vigilant media or active regulators. As such, a politics of responsibility necessarily brings risk and danger. It makes freedom into a weight as well as a release because this is the necessary downside of any political project that is about encouraging people to realize their potential. Without a motivating risk, people and institutions rarely find their best qualities.

Where then does this leave the state itself? One obvious implication is that, if the state does deliberately try to create a more responsible society, a heavy burden falls on its own shoulders. Its own standards of integrity and propriety must be second to none. If it uses its immense power to persuade and to proselytize, it must abide by its own ideas. Otherwise the result is a disastrous corrosion of mutual obligation, a grasping amorality that is one of the bitterest legacies of Stalinism.

The idea of responsibility lends no easy answers. But it does at least ask the pertinent questions. They demand to be addressed because the progressive delinking of power and responsibility brought about by a globalizing market, and more mobile and contingent societies, threatens any philosophy rooted in communality or collectivism. No community can long remain coherent without shared ideals of responsibility. Nor can a society prosper for long if it rewards the irresponsible; if it demoralizes and downgrades those who choose to take on responsibilities instead of financial reward; if it sends signals to schoolchildren that it is better to be a commodities broker or an advertiser of sports cars than a teacher or doctor; and if society encourages, to use Albert Hirschman's distinction, exit in place of voice. If all relationships and obligations are contingent, we can expect that the result will be bad decisions and unwelcome outcomes.

'Responsibility' became a dull and dusty word, a bit too pious for the late twentieth century. Feminists talked about it intermittently, criticizing the male lust for power without responsibility, and contrasting it with the responsibility of reproduction and nurture. The greens raised it if only in relation to the environment. But the left long ago got bored with talking about responsibility, although the individual's sense of being responsible for the fate of others continued to be one of the main motivations for being involved in socialist politics.

While the right flounders between moralism and ultra-libertarianism, between its cult of the individual and its economic umbilical links with the most highly organized forms of global capitalism, the time is ripe to reassert a simple idea, a good litmus test of any policy or reform. Will it encourage people to take more responsibility for their actions? Does it reward people who choose to take on responsibilities for the quality of other people's lives? Perhaps with the slogan 'individual responsibility where possible, collective responsibility where necessary', such tests could become practical. Politics could move one step closer to the tough ethics which seem more meaningful than abstract ideologies, and it could break further from the vested interests whose primary task has always been to save themselves from ever being called to account.

4

WORLDS OUT OF KILTER: THE POLITICS OF BALANCE AND CHANGE

Despite unprecedented prosperity and technological control, the late twentieth century has been characterized by an unmistakable undercurrent of doubt and fear. This uncertain spirit is reflected in the cultural theories of postmodernism, which call into question the very idea of a single truth and a single reading of the world, in the physical sciences' new interest in theories of catastrophe and chaos, concerned with how small causes can have large and unpredictable effects, and in a climate of doubt about the great stories of enlightenment, progress and liberation that defined the politics of an earlier age.

Uncertainty is a product of perpetual change. In the past, and especially in the Marxist tradition, change was associated with predictability, certainty and progress. The transformation of the world, the means and the ends, could be known and understood. After the experiences of the twentieth century it is no longer easy to be certain which particular means will lead to what ends, or whether today's solutions will not turn out to be tomorrow's problems. Change no longer seems to move in a straight line: it zigzags, going back and forth in discontinuous leaps. With unpredictable change comes endemic uncertainty, about everything from culture and truth, to the climate, the air we breathe and the skills we learn. Above all, perhaps, uncertainty fuels the fear that the environment, both natural and human, is changing more rapidly than our means of adapting to it.

Uncertainty makes for a different kind of politics. Some become more cautious, more fearful of the effects of grand designs. Some turn away from politics altogether, towards the everyday and the personal, while for others uncertainty feeds an ever more intense search for the simplest and starkest faiths and certainties, best of all those of fundamental religion.

Yet uncertainty can be a source of strength as well as weakness. By recognizing the limits of our knowledge, we can draw practical lessons about the world, its malleability and its resistance to change. From the recognition that many processes, economic, ecological or social, are beyond any possibility of direct control, a more realistic and defensive radical politics emerges, which, while losing something of the inspirational power of the brave new worlds of 1789, 1848, 1917 or 1968, is more congruent with the reality of modern oppositional politics. For today, shorn of its utopias, the left is most effective when it plays a defensive role, carefully constructing the space for freedom and real life, and protecting people from the dangers of this world, rather than making promises about worlds they have never seen.

The Heritage of Certainty

One hundred years ago history was generally seen as a smooth progress. Whether through evolution or revolution it was a cumulative advance of human capabilities and reason, and a movement away from uncertainties, superstitions and falsehoods into truth and certainty. The left was very much a part of this tradition. It was shaped by that familiar mix of scientific hope and millenarianism, the belief that the world could be built anew, and that people are basically plastic and perfectible.

As refined into the programmes of Social-Democratic and Marxist-Leninist parties, the belief was that power could be used as a tool. Once the working class took over state power, the world could be moulded into an ideal form. Influenced by the optimism of science, there was a widespread belief that all problems could be rationally solved. The social world could be as plastic as the natural world, as susceptible to control.

This perspective had profound implications. One was that under socialism there would be no more dangers. There would be no need for protection from other people or from the state: the state's powers did not need to be balanced by citizens' rights. Often there would be no need even for an army. Utopia is, literally, no place: that is to say, a society without boundaries and therefore without the need for forces to balance those of the enemy. In the dream of international socialism, the problems of danger disappear because there are no longer boundaries and enemies.

Another implication of faith in rational control was the idea that humanity could break free from its limits. Socialism shared with much of capitalist ideology the expectation that we were moving towards a world without scarcities, a world of abundant material goods that would solve the problems of distribution and struggle. This idea, of a world breaking free from limits, is the common heritage of industrial capitalism and socialism, of Lenin, Brunel and Robert Moses. It permeates all the dominant political philosophies. It sustains faith in growth, in science and technology, in grand projects to build tunnels under the sea, to divert rivers and to send rockets into space. It is a faith that is bound up with reason. The world can be changed because it can be clearly understood, mapped and, in the age of the computer, simulated and modelled.

Uncertainty and Imbalance

Today history is as likely to be seen as a cumulative disaster as a steady progress. On the left the turnaround was marked by Walter Benjamin's famous vision of progress as a terrible storm that drives history hurtling backwards, a vast heap of debris accumulating at its feet.[1] This sense of imbalance, a sense of things out of kilter, now separates us from the blithe confidence of the nineteenth century. Today the imbalance may be economic and social, an imbalance of material provision and life opportunity, an imbalance between classes, regions and races. It may be ecological, an imbalance between short-term greed and long-term survival, and it may be psychic or spiritual, an imbalance between inner needs and what is offered by the prevailing culture and mores. Rather than being steady and cumulative, change has come to be seen as destabilizing.

The shift is reflected in disillusion with the dominant political philosophies, and in the various green and New Age movements where there is a strong emphasis on notions of balance, and on the whole rather than the parts. New catchphrases, such as sustainability and the steady-state economy, reflect the concern. The influence of Taoism, Buddhism and Hinduism, and of the deep ecology movement, has also brought a new equation between the wider imbalances of society and personal, psychic imbalances.

Traditional ideas of balance and harmony long ago lost their currency in the world-view of the West. They survive only partially in such pre-industrial creations as the US constitution, devised as a mechanically equilibrating system, balancing executive, legislature and judiciary, or in the economists' bizarrely inappropriate vision of the capitalist economy as a system of general equilibrium.

By contrast, revolutionary capitalism and revolutionary socialism alike have always sought to foster dynamic imbalances, to drive social change or accumulation through difference. For both it is the vanguard groups, those who are marginally ahead, those with an edge, who drive the system, pulling the mass, the average and the ordinary along in their wake. This is the very essence of industrial societies: permanent, cumulative change and the sweeping away of constraints. In the fact of this force, the storm of progress, ideas of equilibrium came to look reactionary and conservative, barriers to the application of reason and progress.

As forces associated with reason and rationality, neither socialism nor capitalism ever suffered from too much doubt about their historic role. Both derived strength from a sense of historical inevitability, a sense that there was no alternative. But in the century of the concentration camp and gulag, the nuclear bomb (built for freedom or for socialism), eugenics and the artificial intelligence guided missile, their certainties have brought a heavy cost. Reason itself has turned out to be a tricky servant, just as power turned out to be a corrupting tool, demanding constant vigilance, care and criticism. During the course of the twentieth century almost every movement and ideology, without exception, has been touched by unforeseen disaster. The good intentions turned out to be a road to hell. Ecological disaster, mass starvation and chronic financial instability are among the costs of 1980s and 1990s global free market capitalism. Genocide turned out to be the destiny of Stalinist communism, of nazism and of the extreme anti-industrial, green ideology of Pol Pot. In each case the revolutionary belief in a single set of universal principles, in the need for a *tabula rasa* to create the world anew, turned out to be profoundly dangerous. In each case, too, ideas were given such weight that there could be no compromise.

These experiences have given us a much stronger sense that limits are an inherent part of the world. The desire to escape from limits seems to bring pathological results, psychic and material costs that show up in unexpected places. We also have a better understanding of the difficult nature of the world and of the problems involved in changing it. And, if there is one unarguable conclusion to be drawn from the experiences of the twentieth century, it is that all systems are imperfect, not just coincidentally but fundamentally. From today's perspective we can see that, for all their subtleties and complexities, the dominant political philosophies of both left and right remained fundamentally one-dimensional and unbalanced. They drew on a set of principles or assumptions about human psychology, selfishness or sociability, to deduce universal principles for living and for organizing societies. All, whether capitalist, socialist, communal or religious, imposed simple structures on to a complex reality. And though all might work well if run by angels, all in practice had to function with human egos, jealousies and prejudices.

The Tradition of Defence

The left paid a particularly heavy price for hopes betrayed, and for its excessive faith in the world's malleability. But it also has another tradition which has been less vulnerable to uncertainties and imbalances. This is the tradition of politics as a defence against danger.

Danger and insecurity are a natural part of the human condition, and much of social life, language itself, rituals and altruisms, can be understood as collective responses to threat. The presence of danger also explains why co-operative, food-sharing creatures have often been favoured over selfish ones in the history of evolution. Danger has also always shaped political discourse, providing justifications for strong leaders, for laws to sustain civil peace, and for rights to defend against the overweening power of states. Danger was also present at the birth of many socialist organizations which were built more as organs of defence than as vehicles to attack and replace the old order. Trade unions and mutual aid societies offered collective protection against a hostile, unpredictable world, food co-operatives defence against hunger, militias defence against professional armies and mercenaries. This idea of defence is also one of the sources of egalitarianism, which arises not from envy or a simple desire for equality, but rather from the experience of subordination and the wish to defend against it.

Today, of course, there are new dangers. The thin envelope of biosphere within which human life takes place suddenly seems extraordinarily vulnerable (though James Lovelock and the proponents of the Gaia thesis might disagree). Nuclear weapons threaten not only human life, but all life through the nuclear winter. Danger is no longer only material and personal, but also macroscopic, a threat to the very idea of living, loving, thinking beings. Other dangers flow from the unstable and uncontrollable nature of global financial markets, from the persistence of nationalisms armed to the teeth, and from the potential access of terrorists to leading-edge armaments. Perhaps the biggest danger of all is the fact that these new dangers are now of a different order than our means of redressing and containing them.

In the past it was the belief in a revolutionary transformation that provided much of the inspiration and vision of socialist and radical movements. In recent years, however, this belief has made the socialist project less relevant to an interconnected world of more porous boundaries, a world of very real limits. It has made it inarticulate in the face of acid rain or AIDS. As a result, there is a striking gap between the power of the left as a radical, oppositional force and its power as a utopian alternative. As an opposition the left plays the role of lookout, warning about dangers, about wars and petty violences, pointing out the costs and limits that lie behind the glossy façade of late twentieth-century capitalism. As a utopian alternative, by contrast, it now seems merely fanciful, wishing away the real problems of the world. Where a century ago the utopias of William Morris and H. G. Wells were bestsellers, the new left utopias of writers like Andre Gorz have little resonance beyond small circles of intellectuals. Instead it is the sense of limits and trade-off, of dangers that capitalism ignores, that has become more potent and that makes people sit up and listen.

Trust and Uncertainty

The left's influence as a warning system feeds on widespread distrust. Where in the past the radicals fed on popular distrust of churches, priests, kings and bosses, today it is the multinational corporation, the government and the bureaucracy that are likely to be distrusted. The widespread predictions made a few decades ago that increasingly sophisticated media and propaganda techniques would produce a passive, credulous and malleable population have been proved wildly wrong. The techniques of information and misinformation, 'swamping', spin control and the calculated leak have all simply engendered greater scepticism about whether anyone can be believed. This has had its impact on the political process, where trust and distrust play an important role. Parties seem to win elections because they are less distrusted than the other side. Within institutions there is a greater stress on structures of accountability to remove leaders for incompetence, betrayal or corruption (on the grounds that power corrupts and absolute power corrupts absolutely).

A similar effect is visible in relation to political systems and ideologies. Nowadays people are much more likely to ask whether they can trust a system to deliver what it promises, and whether they can trust it to relinquish power if it fails. The problem is more acute for some political philosophies than for others. The world's communist movements in particular were irretrievably tainted by their history; having once won power, irreversible structures were created so that they could not be removed.

But the problem of trust is not confined to communism. Similar questions can be asked of neoliberalism and the global market. It is seldom easy, for example, to reverse steps towards marketization when property rights are entrenched, when cultures of public service are destroyed and when individuals defined solely as consumers lose the ability collectively to organize around issues.

It is no coincidence that irreversibility has been an important goal for the new right. In the writings of Friedrich Hayek and others, laws are used to force the replacement of the state by the market, using irreversible constitutional means to minimize the realm of political decision making and take power away from what are seen as irresponsible democratic assemblies. The revolutionary right thus precisely mirrors the left's traditional concern with blocking reaction through irreversible shifts in power.

Both now look equally illegitimate. Today's uncertainties and distrusts suggest that a structure or decision that can be reversed, that leaves us able to change our minds, is inherently better than an irreversible one. Other things being equal, a development that leaves an old community and old architecture intact is better than one that does not; a general skill is better than a specific one that may soon become obsolete; and a political restructuring (perhaps to pass powers to the European Parliament) is better if there is scope for democratically reversing it at a later date.

The idea of reversibility is not new. It is one of the virtues of democratic structures, and the powerful argument against dictatorships and one-party states, unaccountable managers and trade union general secretaries elected for life. But it takes on a new significance when, as now, considerable energy is being spent rectifying old mistakes. We need reversible decisions precisely because we are uncertain about outcomes. For the same reason we need agencies to warn us, to monitor actions, to act as watchdogs, and we need constitutional rights (for workers, consumers and citizens) to balance and limit those in power.

There is also a second implication, equally relevant when policies and programmes are being decided. If we cannot be certain that a system is trustworthy, that our principles are universally applicable, or that our chosen means will deliver the desired ends, then it follows that we should always favour the coexistence of more than one system over just one, however perfect and appealing it may seem.

The coexistence of more than one system reduces the scope for damage when things go wrong; it makes a society better able to adjust to unforeseen circumstances; it creates competition between systems, a competition that can be philosophical as much as economic, forcing each to live up to its ideals, or to adapt; and it gives the individual or group a degree of philosophical choice about the right way to live and work.

Competition in this sense can be read either at a superficial level, as in the social-democratic mixed economy, which was mixed as to ownership rather than ethos, or at a deeper level as competition between different ways of life. Examples from the past might include the coexistence of different monastic orders within a church, offering a range of choice to different types of personality. Present-day examples might include the coexistence of very different approaches to education (traditional and modern, authoritarian and libertarian, religious and secular), of alternative energy sources or transport systems (public, private and community based). Within the economy competing systems might include private enterprises and socialized ones, worker and consumer co-operatives and individual traders, each with a differently structured relationship to capital markets and consumers, and different conceptions about participation in work. Alternatively, they might include competing approaches to health (orthodox, homeopathic) or housing (private, communal, condominiums or public).

Such a pluralism brings with it a distinctive idea of what the state is for. Rather than applying uniform rational principles, its task becomes one of overseeing the balance between systems, redistributing resources and creating the conditions for a variety of groups and institutions to organize themselves. Rather than engaging in social engineering (the old mechanistic metaphor), the state's legitimate task becomes one of creating the space for social experiment.

The idea of competing systems also suggests a distinctive view of change. Where the traditional socialist model of change assumed that the levers of power could be used to realize a blueprint or vision of society, the alternative approach starts from the assumption of weakness rather than strength, defence rather than attack. The aim is not to create society anew but to create balancing forces. Rather than seeking to overthrow hostile forces (the traditional aim of revolutionary movements), the aim is to build up countervailing powers, so as to create a balance of systems, a protection against the danger of any one set of powers or interests becoming too strong. Transformation comes from shifting balances rather than demolition and reconstruction.

Rather than trying to eliminate them, the state therefore aims to create countervailing powers to multinational capital, to the military–industrial complex, or to well-organized professional groups. It balances police rights with those of citizens, those of doctors with those of patients. Rather than trying to resolve inherent conflicts of interest, it creates a new balance between them.

This approach demands a break with old habits of thought. In socialist thought there is a long tradition, with antecedents in millenarian thought, of seeking a final resolution of the world's problems. The individual and the social were to be resolved in a higher synthesis; conflicting class interests were to disappear in a common interest. Today, we are more likely to see conflicts of interest as inevitable in any society: they can be reduced and contained but not eliminated. Philosophically, the point was perhaps best put by Schumacher when he wrote that societies need 'stability and change, tradition and innovation, public interest and private interest, planning and laissez faire, order and freedom, growth and decay. Everywhere society's health depends on the simultaneous pursuit of mutually opposed activities or aims. The adoption of a final solution means a kind of death sentence for man's humanity and spells cruelty or dissolution, generally both'.[2]

These ideas of reversibility and of competing systems pose problems for the socialist traditions, though neither is in any way contrary to their spirit. Both principles are primarily concerned with means rather than ends, a recognition of uncertainty as to which means will achieve which ends, and a recognition that any conscious, participatory society will often change its mind: that the best plans are continuous processes rather than blueprints to be put into practice. Karl Marx, after all, was surely right to retain an intense suspicion of socialist blueprints throughout his life. The future would be forged out of struggle and experience and could not be foreseen.

Variety and Change

The virtues of plural solutions are corroborated by evidence from systems theory and biology. A famous law in cybernetic theory states that any controlling mechanism requires as much variety as the system it seeks to control. According to W. R. Ashby's 'law of requisite variety', it is impossible to control a complex system without an equally complex set of tools. It is, for example, impossible for a government to guide a complex economy simply by using a single measure, such as the money supply or interest rates. Since governments are rarely able to match the complexity of the societies they govern, the implication is that control must be devolved and spread.

Variety also has another value that takes us back to the problems of uncertainty: it allows systems and societies to cope with unforeseen changes. In biology it is well known that species benefit by maintaining a variety of different forms or mutations, so that they are better placed to survive when the environment changes in unpredictable ways. Grasses with the same genetic codes will tend to take a variety of forms, some small, some large, the better to ensure survival in the event of being eaten by animals or starved by drought. In the same way, it is because we do not know which institutions or societies will best respond to a dramatic shift in the climate, to supercomputers the size of a matchbox, or to new, virulent diseases, that we need variety in all the forms of social life, a variety not only in terms of jeans and baked beans but also in terms of systems of meaning.

The failure to understand this, the deeper meaning of variety, is one of the weaknesses of neoliberalism, which offers only one organizing principle for society: the demands of the market, of competitiveness and of a world turned into commodities. The paradoxical effect is to standardize even amid a rhetoric of diversity. All kinds of institutions must be run according to similar principles of management, run 'by the numbers', through accountability to monetary values. And all parts of the world and all spheres of life must be made commensurate within a single system of exchange and value.

Coping with Change

One might expect the left to be more open to diversity and variety since more than ever before it is constituted by many currents and experiences. Yet it still lacks any convincing theories or metaphors for understanding change. The left was brought up always to search for a new steady state (after the revolution or the election of a socialist government), rather than seeing change and adaptation as natural. In this sense, the left shares some of the weaknesses of the modern green movement, with its search for a new, static harmony. Neither fully accepts that change might be continuous and unavoidable, whether it be towards a more ecologically based economy, towards greater material equality or towards a greater realization of human potentials.

The left's view of change is also hampered by the surviving influence of eighteenth- and nineteenth-century views of societies as machines or buildings. In these metaphors, changes came from a new driver or architect and were associated with the certainties of the map and the plan. We are now more likely to recognize that change is by its very nature deeply uncertain and unpredictable. The most appropriate metaphors are now to be found not in physics and mechanics (though physics has had its own sustained encounter with uncertainty), but in the various life sciences, within which change is conceived as a process of searching, and of trial and error.

In the past biological theories of evolution were resisted on the left because of their association with reactionary apologists who used them to legitimate inequalities and hierarchies. 'Organic' views of society denied the reality of conflicting interests. Evolutionary theories seemed to give undue weight to natural processes that are the opposite of the realm of politics, of active choice and determination. But modern evolutionary theories avoid most of these problems (while also giving useful ammunition against racists). Rather than drawing a picture of one-dimensional competition, they view societies as open systems in exchange with their environments, continually adapting and creating new forms of complexity. Some are brilliant but eventually redundant, others functional and effective. Yet it is virtually impossible in advance to predict which will work and which will not.

Much the same is true of innovation in modern economies, so that it should be no surprise that evolutionary theories of this kind are beginning to have an impact on economic theory,[3] challenging the static, ahistorical approaches of neoclassical orthodoxy. In political theory they remain very much on the margins, but in this area too their less mechanistic metaphors offer useful lessons about the nature of change and political transformation. One is the familiar idea that a changing environment requires continual adaptation: a political theory appropriate for the year 2000 will almost certainly be less appropriate in the year 2100. A second is that what marks humans off from other species is the extent to which evolution has to be conscious, however little we understand the environment for which we are trying to evolve: however deep the uncertainties, we have no choice but to plan and to attempt to impose order.

Precisely because of these uncertainties, however, evolution depends on risk, experiment and chance: without random genetic mutation there can be no change (one reason why sexually reproducing creatures, which multiply the scope for mixing and mutation, dominate the world). Similarly, without experiment in the forms of economic life, in family life, in morality and political institutions, without allowing for failure as well as success, societies stop evolving and slip into stagnation.

A fourth lesson follows from the fact that evolution is not synonymous with change. Instead successful evolution is always both conservative and radical. It must be compatible with what goes before it, and if it is too radical the very thing that is being changed falls apart. In the case of political institutions, too much change tends to lead to a crisis of faith and legitimacy. The problems of change arise, both in biology and in political life, because a new environment will tend to throw up more apparent possibilities than are compatible with what has gone before. In the case of a society, there will always be many new ways of doing things that seem to fit the new times but which are too destabilizing to traditions and habits, too threatening to the society's coherence and solidarity. The same is true of political parties, trade unions and voluntary organizations.

Attempting to find this balance is never easy. Different parts move at different speeds, some too fast, too willing to grasp the latest modern thing, some too slow even to see that the world has changed. Obsolescence, a difference in rates of change, is endemic not only for the old but also for the failed avant-gardes and futurisms. Those societies which can encourage a culture of experiment while also minimizing the costs of changing too fast or too slowly will tend to be the ones best able to adapt without losing their basic solidarity and coherence. A society that does not penalize people too heavily for being in a declining region or industry, or for being too far ahead of their time, will tend to be happier than one that does.

These various reflections on uncertainty, balance and change have a common theme. It is that too much certainty, and too much rigidity, is dangerous and disabling. The one-dimensional politics of Marxist-Leninists and free marketeers are best grown out of. In the world of politics and social life – unlike physics – every problem has more than one valid solution.

But there is also another implication for an age beset by uncertainties and dangers, one that goes to the heart of what politics is about. It concerns what we mean by freedom. In a dangerous world of continuous change, freedom must mean more than the absence of restraints, a freedom for dynamic enterprise or personal hedonism. Emancipation is not enough. Instead freedom comes to mean something different: a safe zone for autonomy and real life, protected from an array of threatening forces, from concern about air or water, from the need to sell oneself on the labour market, from prejudices and oppressions. In a highly interconnected and interdependent world, few things are more vital than that freedom for real life be carefully guarded, not only from physical threats but also from other people's excessive certainties.

Notes

1 Walter Benjamin, *Illuminations: theses on the philosophy of history*, Fontana, London, 1970.
2 E. F. Schumacher, *A Guide for the Perplexed*, Abacus, London, 1977, p. 127.
3 An impressive recent attempt to apply these metaphors to economics can be found in G. Dosi *et al.*, *Technical Change and Economic Theory*, Frances Pinter, London, 1988.

5

WHAT IS TELEVISION FOR? THE PURSUIT OF QUALITY

Television has become overwhelmingly the dominant medium of the late twentieth century: the paramount place where elections are conducted and where fictions are disseminated. How it is run, by whom and in what interests, is arguably a more important issue for any modern society than control over major industries, the law or finance.

Yet political theorists remain little interested in how it works, and little thought has been given to what a good broadcasting system would look like beyond a rather obvious assumption that it should be impartial and honest. In this essay I set out a framework for thinking about television's qualities: its role as an economic good and as an aesthetic; its relationship to citizenship and communities, to ideas of the good life and pluralism. I also attempt the more controversial, but I believe unavoidable, task of explaining how a television system can be adequate to its society, and the criteria by which it should be judged.

More than half a century after the first broadcasts there are few things we can say with much certainty about television. We know that it is expensive to make (hundreds of thousands of pounds an hour for dramas and programmes like *Miami Vice*) and extremely cheap to receive. We know that on average British people watch over twenty-five hours each week, between a third and a half of their free time, in the USA rather more and in most other countries rather less, and we know that the heaviest watchers are the young and the old. We know that most people watch primarily for entertainment, escape and relaxation, to 'fill in the gaps in the day', and that although television remains the most authoritative source of news, its role as an informer and educator remains secondary. And we know something about the make-up of audiences, though television audiences remain far less segmented than those for other media.

Beyond these and a few other accepted truths one enters the realm of opinion and argument. No one really knows what effects television has on its audience, whether it is an effective ideological indoctrinator, whether it promotes violence and antisocial behaviour or a healthy curiosity about other people's lives. There is less agreement about what television could or should be for – inducing docility, expanding awareness, purveying harmless trivia, or contributing to exports – than there is about almost any major institution. Worse, throughout the Western world it is hard to find any common vision about its long-term evolution, whether it be towards a smooth extension of the public service status quo, narrowcasting, interactivity, a multiplicity of televisions (business TV, educational TV, etc.) or towards ever more sophisticated technologies of high definition and video hypertext.

This essay is concerned with another area of opinion: perhaps the one issue in broadcasting that resists a definitive and rational answer more than any other; the one issue which should be of concern to everyone with an interest in how the society works. This is the question of quality, of what constitutes good television.

During the 1980s and 1990s quality has become the core of the debate about television, the point which every claim had to touch. The same has been true in many other fields. Throughout political and social life concern about quality has returned: the quality of life, of the environment and of products are all seen as legitimate areas of political debate. Quality and excellence have also become the holy grail in business life, the solution to problems of competitiveness, motivation and innovation.

In broadcasting, as elsewhere, quality is one of those things that it is very hard to be against. Yet it has been significant that two of the most influential groups thinking about television have deliberately argued that judgements of quality have no place in the debate. For the liberal economists who have driven the debate on both sides of the Atlantic it is of far less interest than market structure and efficiency, or for that matter the freedom to buy, sell and publish. For them most arguments about quality are little more than the special pleading of vested interests, fearful that their restrictive cartels are soon to be bust open. Meanwhile for many of the television academics, particularly those influenced by semiotics, postmodernism and the new schools of cultural studies, quality is a non-issue for another reason, namely that it is just another legitimation of the old hierarchies of judgement, a concept drained of meaning by years of use by those in power.

There is no escaping the strength of these arguments. In Britain, perhaps more than anywhere else, a rhetoric of quality in broadcasting has consistently been used to legitimize, and disguise, the narrow tastes and prejudices of a small, metropolitan, cultural elite. In broadcasting as in the visual arts, theatre and opera, ideas of quality, taste and aesthetics often seem to work more as social markers, a means of asserting superiority and difference, than as in any way neutral or objective. This is one reason why today's use of the word 'quality' as an uncontroversial synonym (or rather codeword) for public service is so problematic: it simply obscures the very real weaknesses of the public service tradition.

But these arguments take us only so far. The critique of quality always runs the risk of simply abdicating responsibility, vacating an important area of cultural argument. It leaves a lingering sense of unease, because some judgements, whether individual or collective, are inescapable in any society. So although it is impossible to arrive at any final definition of quality – it is one of the political philosopher's 'essentially contestable concepts' – it remains important to try to establish criteria, aesthetic or otherwise, for judging television.

Part of the reason is that criticism and judgement are part of the very process of making television, just as they are in any other public activity. If critics and audiences do not repeatedly criticize programmes, developing a more sophisticated armoury with which to judge, then it is all too likely that standards will slip, that bad television will displace the good. In precisely the same way, a political class that does not include perceptive critics, able to judge the craft and skill of politicians, will find that its standards fall. Indeed, the price of the conservatism inherent in any consistent criteria of judgement is well worth paying, for a society that loses interest in arguing about the qualities of its media, or for that matter the quality of its buildings, working environments and countryside, is becoming emptier, poorer and less alive.

Audiences and Quality

If you ask those involved in broadcasting what they mean by quality, the answers you get will be at best vague and at worst muddled.[1] Quality will be equated with everything from diversity to non-trivialization, significance to sympathy. it is taken to be that which 'enhances the total life of the community'. You will find it widely assumed that quality can be equated with social class. As in the word's archaic meaning (when quality referred to social rank), quality broadcasting, like the quality press, is simply that which people of 'quality' enjoy.[2]

An alternative starting point has been to ask viewers what they think about quality. This is a valuable exercise, though its results are ambiguous. Audience appreciation indices (AIs), for example, provide a good measure of audience perceptions of quality, offering an alternative to the stale debate between a crude populism ('ten million viewers can't be wrong') and an equally crude elitism ('ten million viewers will almost certainly be wrong'). It is certainly true that AIs reveal just how many small audience programmes (ranging from 'hobby' programmes to dramas and cult comedies) have very enthusiastic audiences. Strikingly, they reveal that there is sometimes an almost inverse relationship between AIs and ratings.

That said, however, any detailed study of AIs shows both that they are rarely very sensitive and that enjoyment and quality are far from closely related. The appreciation associated with a football win for the home side gives little insight into how well it was filmed. Similarly, new programmes tend to have lower AI ratings than older and more established ones. Aggregate AI figures may disguise the very high appreciation of one part of the audience. So although AI figures provide some insights into viewer perceptions, particularly as they change over time, they are far from being a definitive answer to the problem of quality.

Probe a bit deeper and you find that there are very complex attitudes at work.[4] Many feel obliged to agree with the dominant definitions of quality, those defined by the broadcasters. Yet even though for most people 'quality simply means good – that which they enjoy',[5] when surveyed people consistently felt the need to criticize the quality of the very programmes they enjoyed. In one study, for example, 73 per cent saw soap operas, including the glossy US imports like *Dallas* and *Dynasty*, as the obvious examples of 'poor quality' programming, yet when they were asked which programmes they most enjoyed, soap operas dominated the list. David Morley, one of the most astute commentators on the everyday uses of television, has written that women in particular 'often displayed guilt when talking about their pleasures in watching romance or soap opera material on television'.[6] The discussion of quality, it would seem, has been constrained by an overbearing conventional wisdom.

I cite this example solely to suggest how complex the question of quality is. Like all modern social issues it is reflexive – bound up with social self-understanding and misunderstanding. It is for that very reason that broadcasting quality is not an issue of concern only to broadcasters and their viewers. Rather broadcasting's values are extrinsic as well as intrinsic, so that although there is a use for purely aesthetic arguments about particular programmes or channels, any serious debate about broadcasting cannot avoid looking at its place in society, the society's virtues and ills, its most effective modes of organization, and the degree to which it shares common interests.

This is a key point, and one that is lost when the debate about quality focuses only on programmes. The most important question we need to ask of any broadcasting system is whether it is adequate for its society: does it really reflect and express its experiences, its pleasures and pains, its insights and understandings, its differences as well as its similarities? Does it function adequately as a set of channels for groups and individuals to communicate to each other? The same questions could be asked of a society's literature or music, but they become unavoidable for television simply because it absorbs so much of our time, money and interest, and because its central political status makes judgements inescapable.

This essay maps out seven ideas of quality, some familiar, some less so. The aim is to show that all ideas of quality carry with them a heavy baggage of philosophical assumptions: about the nature of the medium, the purposes of society and the nature of the people who watch. These assumptions clash, conflict and contradict. Such tensions are inevitable in a society where there is no longer a clear consensus about freedoms and rights, about 'moral standards' or about the relationship of the individual to the community. In a heterogeneous society an adequate broadcasting system must retain a diversity of qualities. The greatest dangers emerge only when one view or interest (that of financial backers, politicians, advertisers, moral regulators or broadcasters themselves) crowds out all the others.

Producer Quality and Professionalism

In Britain the discourse on quality has traditionally been dominated by programme makers. It can be called the tradition of producer quality. Quality is seen in terms of production values as defined by the community of producers, which includes the writers, directors and editors. It is concerned with technical issues of lighting, camera work, script and direction, the quality of acting, and the effectiveness with which ideas are conveyed or with which a narrative is unravelled. It takes its purest form in the classic ingredients of quality drama (the very pinnacle of 'quality television'): expensive looking productions (but without vulgar special effects), well-known actors and actresses with theatrical pedigree, and literary resonance in the subject matter.

Though the literary drama is its purest expression, the conventional wisdom also has wider currency. At its heart is the idea that there is a set of aesthetic values which are, in principle, applicable to any kind of television. These values work alongside a craft view of television, which judges programmes by the success with which they are innovative and creative within the given conventions and rules of the medium.

I have called this approach 'producer quality' because it is the producers who guard it. In another medium the critics might play this role. In literature and film, for example, there is a small army of critics who take it on themselves to spot new talent, to judge the good, the bad and the indifferent. Television criticism, by contrast, has a relatively low status, varying between simple pre-viewing and the use of programmes as a peg for witty commentary. Television critics become famous, if at all, because they are entertaining to read, not because of the insights they offer.

In television, then, it is the makers themselves who guard the medium's most essential values. They bring to this role several different ways of thinking about quality. Alongside the first definition of quality, which judges it by a universal set of rules, an alternative approach sees it as something that exists within forms or genres: there is a best in everything from middle-of-the-road rock to avant-garde theatre, and each requires its own appropriate kinds of criticism. So although there is no way of comparing a soap opera and a documentary, we can judge each by reference to the grammars and traditions of its form. Again this idea of quality tends to be defined by the community of producers involved in each genre or form.

Both approaches leave to the programme makers the task of distinguishing good and bad. Ideologically, both bring with them a strong commitment to producer autonomy. Like the author or artist, the producer alone must be responsible for the creative process: any concession either to the higher echelons of the bureaucracy or to the pressures of the market is undesirable. Independence, whether guaranteed through the size and stature of an organization like the BBC, or through the (apparent) economic independence of an independent, is at a premium. Moreover, although the reality of television is, of course, very different from this, all production being highly co-operative and dependent on a multitude of compromises (Anthony Smith has written that there is 'no concept more intractable than "creative freedom"'), the important point is the strength of the ideal.

It has to be noted that this ideal is far from democratic in spirit: as Edward Buscombe has written, 'it is a question not only of the freedom from interference above, but also the "freedom" to control those below'.[7] Creative freedom and the defence of quality are generally seen as a prerogative of managers, directors and producers, who live by a professional ethos that is one of the distinctive features of British broadcasting. Unusually, the production function is buried within the managerial process: British 'management tends to have far more collective experience in production itself than in ... foreign systems'.[8]

British broadcasting has always ridden a tension between wishing to break free from its constraints to become art, and the reality of being a highly industrial production process. According to Anthony Smith, the producer works, paradoxically, 'as a kind of "author" directly inside a manufacturing and distribution process'. This tension is only partly resolved by new technologies which help to flatten the organizational pyramid, blurring the division of labour and allowing, at least potentially, for more direct authorial control. Digital editing, electronic news gathering technologies' computerized lighting set-ups, remote control of cameras and paintboxes are all obvious examples. In practice however, everyone works within a context. Free expression and professional autonomy turn out to depend far more on the prevailing culture, on the generosity of funds, than on the overt relationships between administrators and creators.

In today's debates about broadcasting, the most eloquent representatives of British television, brought up within this tradition of professional autonomy, argue that producer sovereignty has produced the best television in the world, simultaneously innovative, challenging and popular. Television is safe in its own hands, leading and responding to popular interests while also developing the art of the medium. It is precisely this sovereignty of professional producers that is held to protect it from the bland commercialism of the cinema and the lower depths and owner manipulation of the press. Like an administrative cadre, the broadcasters present themselves as an interest above interest. Their freedom of expression is the guarantee of diversity and quality for the viewer.

Consumer Quality and the Market

Against producer sovereignty stands what is now the equally familiar claim for consumer sovereignty, usually propounded not by consumers themselves, but by other producers seeking entry to the marketplace. The last twenty years have seen a striking shift in the balance of the argument. Where in the 1960s and 1970s discussion of broadcasting concerned itself with the ethos and responsibilities of a profession, and with its modes of representation, its access and accountability, today's debate is primarily about business, competition and profitability. At the level of rhetoric at least, the centre of gravity has shifted from the producer to the consumer. Changing technologies have provided part of the push. The multiple channels of cable and DBS make television much more like other markets where consumers can regulate the quality and appropriateness of what is produced. Pay-per-view, pay channels, interactivity and the various technologies ranging from addressable converters to video-on-demand all promise the viewer much greater choice and control.

The change also reflects another material reality. The economic pressures on broadcasting, and particularly the BBC, and the growing weight of independent producers running small businesses, have made many broadcasters far more aware of economic and commercial realities. The need to satisfy an audience has become that much more important. But the change also reflects the influence of a small number of economists, notably Sir Alan Peacock, Sam Brittan, Charles Jonscher and Cento Veljanovski. Their arguments are founded almost entirely on neoclassical economics' ideal of consumer sovereignty. Not that there is much overlap with the modern consumer movement. It is hard not to be struck by the remarkable gap between the agenda of modern consumerism – producer obligation, honest representation, quality and standards – and that of the economists, whose abstract consumers are much less flesh and blood than the ones who really watch television. But the important point is that the consumer has moved to centre stage: everyone claims to speak for the viewer, and everyone wishes to mobilize viewers behind their own ideas and interests.

In relation to quality, the 'consumer' argument comes in 57 varieties. The crudest (and most familiar) argues that the only useful notion of quality is that which identifies it with the preferences of viewers. The most popular programme is to all intents and purposes the best. Questions of quality may be of intellectual interest, but they should not play any role in shaping institutions and policies. As Mark Fowler, the former Chairman of the US Federal Communications Commission, put it: 'instead of defining public demand and specifying categories of programming to service this demand', regulators 'should rely on broadcasters' ability to determine the wants of their audiences through the mechanisms of the marketplace'.[9] Any alternative definition of quality, especially when it seeks to influence which programmes are made, automatically implies the imposition of one person's subjectivity over another, usually that of a metropolitan elite on to the population at large. The consumer argument is implicitly relativistic: each to his own, *de gustibus non est disputandum*, and so on.

The argument derives much of its energy from being an attack on a privileged elite. In Britain, critiques of this kind were usually made from the left. Quality was seen as one of the excuses used to block wider access to the medium. Professionalism served as a barrier to democratization. Engineering standards were also seen to serve a political purpose. On radio, for example, arguments for technical quality were used to deny access to tapes made by oral history or community groups. The need for transmission quality served as an excuse to prevent licensing of community stations. In general, arguments for quality were seen as tools used to preserve broadcasting for the world-view of a sophisticated upper-middle class, a means of airbrushing out the rough edges and conflicts of the wider world.

In the 1980s and 1990s the critique of quality tended to come from the right. At the 1989 Edinburgh Television Festival, Rupert Murdoch argued that 'much of what is claimed to be quality television here is no more than the parading of the prejudices and interests of [these people] . . . [and] has had . . . debilitating effects on British society, by producing a TV output which is so often obsessed with class, dominated by anti-commercial attitudes and with a tendency to hark back to the past'.

Significantly, the clarion call for a shift to market principles and consumer sovereignty is bound up with a set of ideas about the purposes of television, the values and virtues it should endorse. The call for deregulation summons to its aid the arguments of people like Martin Wiener and Corelli Barnet about the historic failure of the British ruling class. Television is asked to dethrone its own rulers so that it can act as an agent of modernization, pulling its weight in the creation of an enterprise culture.

The more sophisticated versions of the argument to 'give the people what they want' recognize that the links between supply and demand are less simple than those operating in the market for clothes or even books. For a start there is no simple market relationship between producers and users (the key economic relationships are between advertisers and broadcasters, and between the BBC and the government, which sets and collects the licence fee). There is a huge gulf between the value of the service that viewers receive and the money they spend on it, whether directly or indirectly (which explains the frenetic zeal of cable, satellite and video companies to tap this latent source of revenue).

It is also well known that the bald audience figures that interest advertisers can disguise very different intensities of pleasure or satisfaction. For the economically literate there is a recognition that the peculiar economies of scale in broadcasting bias against small audiences, or unusually localized tastes (this is particularly true when most viewers can receive only a handful of channels). Others have pointed out that many of those most dependent on television – the old, the unemployed, the housebound – make up the audiences that advertisers are least interested in reaching. All of these features of the televisual world make it harder to pretend that unadulterated markets can be relied on to maximize consumer satisfaction.

There are also more fundamental economic reasons for doubting how far television can, or should, be turned into a common or garden commodity. Because marginal costs of reception verge towards zero, there are strong arguments for believing that the maximization of consumer utility is better achieved by financing a universally available service through a licence fee, than by providing a subscription service to 20 or 50 per cent of the population.[10] Similar arguments have been used to justify subsidizing cabling schemes (the costs of cabling two-thirds of the houses in a street are not twice those of cabling one-third). The peculiar economics of broadcasting, which are nearer to those of the air than to those of the paperback book, lend strong support to the social and cultural arguments advanced for keeping broadcasting 'free at the point of consumption'.

Those arguing the free market case for restructuring broadcasting have often accepted that certain kinds of programme should be insulated from market forces. In some cases there may be an inherent value in producing particular programmes, whether or not people choose to watch them. Hence the argument made by Samuel Brittan and Alan Peacock, for a market system augmented by public funding of programme categories which are deemed worthwhile because of their quality, but which are unlikely to survive in the cut and thrust of the marketplace. Certain kinds of cultural programme, and some news and documentary services, are usually the obvious candidates, seen as separate from the bulk of broadcasting because of their special qualities. Public service becomes an enclave (an oasis or ghetto depending on one's view) within a market-based system.

A similar conclusion can be reached through an alternative view of consumer quality that is sometimes implicit in recent debates. According to this view, which has its roots in literary theory, quality exists within an economy of demands and rewards. The best-quality television, like the best music or literature, often demands a high investment of time and attention from the viewer, and in turn provides a higher level of reward. The extent to which it is demanding provides a pointer to its quality. The dynamics of the marketplace, of channel hopping and grazing, bias against this kind of broadcasting. Hence the need for special measures to support it (perhaps through subsidies for arts channels) so that consumer welfare can be maximized.

In these various economistic approaches, the value provided by television is understood as a utility that can be compared with other utilities gained through the purchase of food, clothes, videos or cars. The only relevant qualities are those that can be measured through the willingness of an audience to pay more for one programme than for another (a difficult measurement to make, since only a very small proportion of the British population pays directly for any channels or programmes). This need not mean that all programmes must compete as entertainment. A programme that provides viewers with new knowledge, whether of a foreign language, of Italian opera or of how to mend a carburettor, may have more value and quality than the most sumptuously produced costume drama.

Although quality is a rather soft concept for a discipline that is always striving for the hard rigour of a science, economics does have some useful insights to offer. One is the idea of non-price competitiveness. A product that is of higher quality (or more reliable) than another, otherwise comparable product will be competitive even if costs and prices are otherwise the same. Like all the cultural industries, broadcasting is dominated by non-price competition, since there is rarely any clear correlation between underlying costs and the price, value or quality of what is sold. The important point for the purposes of this argument is that the same qualities that may be argued for on cultural grounds can in the right circumstances take on an economic value. A 'Marks & Spencer' approach, which exploits a reputation for quality across a range of products, is particularly attractive. In the case of British broadcasting, the favoured strategy has been to cultivate the classic English look, of literary adaptations based around the lives of the upper middle classes and aristocracy, usually set in the heyday of Empire. The Chief Executive of the BBC's tellingly named US subsidiary, Lionheart Television, has described the BBC strategy as one of improving 'the branding of the BBC label', which 'has come to stand for programmes of special distinction like *Six Wives of Henry VIII*'.[11] Through this and parallel strategies, British broadcasting aims to win an allure and brand power akin to that of IBM in computers or Parker in pens.

Strategies of this kind often depend on the fact that consumers have only limited information about what is available. Because consumers cannot know in advance the quality of a particular programme, they depend on reputation to give some guidance. Reputation becomes an extremely valuable asset. The need to maintain it gives producers an incentive to strive for the highest possible quality. But economic theory also shows that the same factors that promote quality can also undermine it. The famous theory of 'lemons'[12] shows just how easily standards can slip, and how hard it is for the consumer to avoid being taken for a ride. Lemons are products, like the secondhand car (or the film, or television programme), where buyers cannot observe the product's quality prior to purchase. In such markets, there is always an incentive 'for sellers to reduce quality and take short run gains before buyers catch on'.[13] Such is the experience of the cheap and shoddy second and third sequel of the blockbuster film. The problem is accentuated in broadcasting because viewers have only a vague idea of the origin of programmes (a large majority of viewers of that classic of 'quality television', *The Jewel in the Crown*, wrongly believed it to have been made by the BBC). In such markets the individual producer has an incentive to cut costs and quality, since this adversely affects the reputation of television as a whole rather than that of the individual programme or channel.

These arguments can be overplayed. But they do help to explain why so many audiences in countries undergoing broadcast deregulation have experienced a decline in standards and even a sense of being misled and cheated. The familiar demon of consumer dissatisfaction soon appears on the other side of the free market.

Quality and the Medium: Television's Aesthetic

There are many flaws endemic to any view of television which starts with the viewer or the consumer. Perhaps the most fundamental is the assumption that viewers come to television with fully formed tastes and preferences. Television is mistakenly seen as a receiver rather than a shaper of culture and value. The obvious philosophical flaws of this view combine with a deeper failing: seeing television as 'market led' frees broadcasters from any responsibility for their output. The satisfaction of existing needs and demands, however warped, can be seen as morally neutral.

Even more than the producer approach, the consumer philosophy of quality avoids asking too many questions about the purpose of broadcasting, and its place in society. The only exceptions come when libertarian principles are suddenly jettisoned to make room for controls over sex and violence. Otherwise, like the rights and bona fides of professional broadcasters, the rights of consumers exercised in the marketplace are held to be incontestable.

The third set of definitions covers various approaches to quality which start not with the producer or the viewer, but with the intrinsic nature of the medium. They, too, exclude questions about the wider role of broadcasting. Instead they seek a televisual aesthetic, a set of rules of judgement similar to those which might be applied to a film or a book. Unlike the producer definitions of quality, these approaches seek a more objective and distanced aesthetic.

One might expect to gain some insight from the work of the many television academics who have come to prominence around the world in the last twenty years. As I have already mentioned, however, for many of the most influential quality has been something to be attacked rather than investigated. It is interesting, if at all, only as ideology, one that is rooted in the histories of domination by class, gender and nation.

Television studies was founded in the desire to accept and embrace popular television and popular culture, a part of academia's widespread reaction against Leavisite literary theory. From there the need to step away from programmes towards a greater interest in how audiences construct meanings out of programmes was self-evident. Within this paradigm it did not really matter whether a programme was good or bad, whether it was truthful or false. The critical function came to revolve around dissection and deconstruction rather than judgement. Only in the last few years has the fashion begun to shift again as academics found themselves inadvertently allying themselves with the new television moguls. So aesthetics is back, but still without any consensus about how it should be philosophically grounded.

There are several possible starting points. Many people implicitly judge quality in terms of the durability and timelessness of what is produced. The best television is non-ephemeral, taking on some of the properties of literature or film: television is best, in other words, when it escapes from and transcends its instantaneous, transient nature. This view serves as a reminder of television's characteristically parasitic relationship to other media, not only drawing on them for products (the music hall, private-eye detective genre, Hollywood cinema, West End theatre) but also using their legitimacy to bolster its own. This is most strikingly clear when television parades its great literary adaptations, or when television news unquestioningly adopts the agendas of the national press. The dependence on the conventions of pre-television forms is also reflected in the remarkable fact that so many television writers have become famous (David Mercer, John McGrath, Galton and Simpson, Carla Lane, Denis Potter) while their producers and directors remain anonymous. In cinema, by contrast, the position is reversed, though the ideology of the visual author is if anything stronger.

Instead of seeking durability, a diametrically opposite view sees quality in terms of television's ability to be true to its nature as a medium, a nature which is instant, superficial and, in the extreme view, a mere diversion or visual wallpaper. The best television is that which avoids the temptation to be like literature, but which produces the most effective surface effects. The £500,000 advertisement and the pop video, or for that matter the flows of an MTV or 'Night network,' are abvious examples.

The tension between these two views, the one stressing timelessness, the other ephemerality, is apparent in many areas. An obvious example is in the television criticism offered by the press: for the mainstream press, TV criticism is generally written by people from literary backgrounds, with a jokey tone that reflects the view that television is an essentially parasitic, secondary medium, inherently incapable of competing with the acres of newsprint devoted to books or plays. In the newer television criticism, by contrast, found in some of the more avant-garde magazines, television's output is seen as a postmodern swirl of disconnected images which leaves the critic to construct and deconstruct at will.

Both, perhaps, subscribe to the view expounded by Neil Postman[14] that the real 'metalanguage' of television is entertainment, and that the nature of the medium inevitably trivializes issues, blunting any educational effect. However, where the postmodernist welcomes the sea of competing texts, Postman views the overabundance of information as an appalling problem. Instead of information taking on a meaning within one's life and actions, everything is reduced to the need to pass time in as entertaining a fashion as possible. Postman reminds us of Aldous Huxley's fear that big brother will come with a smiling face, actively solicited by the audience. This is the McLuhanite argument against the free market. Precisely because of television's nature as a medium, consumer sovereignty will be a road to hell, the erosion of responsibility and relevance.

Umberto Eco has offered an interesting alternative to this view of television as the destroyer of meaning. Eco proposes an aesthetic that rejects the modernist obsession with innovation and novelty, and its association of quality with the high information content of the new. Instead, in an uncertain and unstable age, he argues that it should not be surprising that people are attracted to the repetitive nature of many of those forms of television that are so often seen as the enemy of quality: the formulaic and predictable soap opera, sitcom and game show have qualities which should not be underestimated. A similar view was proposed by Horace Newcomb[15] when he suggested that a televisual aesthetic should emphasize the virtues of intimacy and continuity. A serial or repetitive aesthetics of this kind has a long pedigree stretching back to ancient Greece, when art and craft were indistinguishable. When creative work revolved around the reworking of familiar grammars and themes, *ars* and *techne* could both be used to describe creative work.[16] For Eco, then, true quality depends on keeping faith with the tradition rather than sweeping it away. An aesthetics appropriate for television must consciously set itself against the prevailing fashion for experiment and change for its own sake.

The work of another continental theorist, Pierre Bourdieu, also offers some insight into why it has proved so hard to develop a consistent aesthetic for television. Bourdieu counterposes what he calls the popular aesthetic, concerned with practicality and usefulness, with sensuality, warmth and gaiety, to the high aesthetic of distinction, difference and hostility to the world of results. The popular aesthetic focuses on the function of television: on whether it entertains or informs, on whether a comedy is funny, or whether a thriller thrills. For a truly refined high aesthetic, by contrast, the best television is that which experiments with form (a Denis Potter play, perhaps). These two aesthetics play very different social roles in everyday life, as well as being rooted in historic differences of class and cultural capital. In Britain, for example, the distinction between the popular and the high aesthetic is bound up with the historic struggle between a populist, classless American television (seen as part of the entertainment industry, show biz, etc.) and a much more class-based English (rather than British) television with aspirations to art and seriousness.

The persistent conflict between the two is all too apparent in television, and in the attitudes of those working within it. Those working on soap operas and game shows, for example, have a very different conception of their role, and of what constitutes success, than those working on drama or arts programmes. Both are bound up in their own, irreconcilable aesthetics.

But Bourdieu takes the argument one step further, suggesting that it might be impossible to develop aesthetic rules for any mass medium. In his classic book *Distinction*,[17] he distinguishes between what he calls the naïve gaze and the pure (or aesthetic) gaze. This opposition is used as part of his more general argument about how culture is used as a tool of social differentiation. In the case of a particular book or piece of music, enjoyment for some people is tied to the fact that other people will view it as alien. Taste and quality work as social markers rather than having an objective basis. The pure gaze, that of the cultivated, sophisticated arbiters of culture, defines itself by its opposition to the simplicities of the popular.

The important point for the present argument is that television's nature as a mass medium, and as a medium of the naïve gaze, may make it inherently unsuitable for the development of an aesthetic. Though different individuals can use television in very different ways, it is much harder to use the medium as a social marker than it is to use one's appreciation of Italian opera or vintage wine. Instead it is easier to define an aesthetics by its opposition to television, a solution that many people in practice choose to adopt.

Perhaps the one field of television that appears to escape these conundrums is actuality. Television can escape from the problems of aesthetics only when it erases its nature as a medium and offers unmediated access to such things as sport and political events: television becomes a window on the world. It offers objective truths (the news has traditionally been the one programme without credits), without authorship. As in some of the early accounts of photography, it is precisely this absence of creative authorship, this distance from the realm of aesthetics, that renders television useful.

Television as Ritual and Communion

Most theories of communication understand it as the passage of images or information from one place to another. What is of interest is the shaping of the message, the ability of the receiver to receive, and the nature of what is transmitted. An alternative view, particularly associated with the American writer James Carey,[18] sees communication as primarily ritualistic. Drawing on the common etymology of 'communication', 'communion' and 'community', it stresses the ways in which communication is bound up with sharing, fellowship and participation. Meanings flow less from a particular programme or channel than from the whole system of communication, its historic cultural traditions and its political economy. All must be understood as elements in a search for shared meanings. Broadcasting itself must be understood less as a means of transmitting images from producers to consumers than as a means of creating a common experience for millions of people living together in a nation or community. The work of Paddy Scannell on 'the communicative ethos' and the place of the question 'did you see?' has also illuminated this, the social context of television.[19]

Understood as a kind of ritual, the form of television is as important as its content. The feeling of communication is more important than the message. The purpose of television is simply to create a community of watchers, engaged in the same activity in real time, sharing experiences, fictions or characters. In the same way, the value of newspapers and records can be found not just in the information or pleasure that they give people, but also in their ability to offer a sense of membership, a means of access to the kinds of relationship with other people that become harder to forge in a less rooted society.

Seeing television as primarily ritualistic lends a very different meaning to the word 'quality'. Rather than having any intrinsic qualities, the quality of a particular piece of television is its ability to carry this role, its ability to define and bind a community. At certain times a particular programme will resonate in this ritual way, throwing ideas and phrases into everyday useage. These programmes will be the ones with th highest quality, as they serve to crystallize a community. Programmes ranging from the Coronation to Live Aid, *Boys from the Blackstuff* to *Cathy Come Home*, or for that matter a royal wedding, become examples of the highest-quality television not because of their art, or even the size of their audience, but because of their role within the history of the community they serve.

Perhaps the most important quality that television has in this view is its democratic, levelling character. When it is universally and freely available, it embodies communitarian, egalitarian values not present in other areas. Whatever is on the screen is visible to all, regardless of wealth or class.

Clearly, there are many different interpretations of the ritual view. There are competing definitions of community: the community of the nation, for example, may be oppressive to those excluded from its history and culture. There is often something very conservative about the use of television to mould a coherent mass out of a diversity of experiences and interests. The ritual view reflects rather than resolves the conflicts that lie under the surface of any society. But in an era when broadcasting is set for rapid change, the question of its ritual function is more pertinent than ever. The move away from three or four channels to fifty or a hundred will make television less important precisely because it will erode the ritual function it now has. The question 'did you see?' may drop out of everyday use. If this does happen, television will lose one of its qualities, one of the ways in which it creates meaning for viewers.

The imminent changes in broadcasting also pose a deeper question. If in an age of multichannel broadcasting, television loses its ritual role, if there is no longer a forum where millions of people congregate in a shared experience, then the medium inevitably becomes part of a challenge to the very idea of a society that is more than an aggregation of its parts. At the extreme, it begins to threaten the moral coherence that any society needs in order to survive.

In the past television has been remarkably effective as a medium of ritual and social solidarity. More than in any other medium there is a remarkable homogeneity of audiences across different types of programme and channel. The segmentation and specialization that many predicted as an effect of many channels has been surprisingly slow to arrive. Television remains a uniting, bridging medium, a common experience that ignores the barriers of class, race and gender. This is why the ritual view of television has a direct relevance for policy. As innumerable alternatives now present themselves to policy makers, it becomes important to ask how much this ritual, binding role should be valued, to make some judgement about the costs of fragmentation.

It is already possible to detect the first signs of a seismic shift in attitudes. On the left the earlier belief that every community needed its own space, its own media and its own arts to explore experiences has been qualified by a greater concern for communication across social boundaries and the use of culture and language as integrating forces. On the right, too, the naive libertarianism of much of the new right is increasingly tempered by a concern for the values of citizenship and the coherence of the nation, again linked to questions of culture and language. The ritual or 'communion' idea of television retains its potency because the futuristic visions of narrowcasting, personalized TV and 'demassification', visions of atomized societies, no longer look quite as attractive as they once did.

Television and the Person

The ritual view judges television by the standards and needs of a community. Television's values and qualities depend on how we value the various communities of which we are members, and on the role it plays in cementing them. A related set of ideas about quality derive from different conceptions of the person, of what it means to be a good, mature, fully formed human being. Rather than seeing all subjectivities as equally valid (the view generally implicit in the economic and consumer approaches), the various strands of this argument are all confident enough to make the claim that some kinds of behaviour are better than others.

The first centres around the idea of citizenship and rights. It asserts the value of public life in relationship to a medium historically associated with the privacy of the 'pleasures of the hearth' and the living room. Seen from this tradition, the good life is that of the active citizen, fully aware of the political and social life of the community, and actively engaged with it. Television is seen as an 'informational commons' which citizens depend on to explain the workings of society and the experiences of others. It helps viewers to participate as fully formed social beings, better able to control their own destiny. Television acts, too, as the tribunal where citizens call their rulers to account, and where investigative journalists uncover malpractices. By its nature it is a democratic medium (available to all), but it also functions as a democratic forum, parallel to the formal ones of a parliamentary democracy, providing a public sphere of argument and debate, often superior to those sustained by the press, political parties and voluntary organizations.

The citizenship arguments clearly stand against the marketization of television, which might imply, for example, well-funded news and current affairs services available only on subscription channels. Two very different ideas of free flow are in play here. Where the free marketeers emphasize freedom of expression, arguments based on citizenship stress freedoms and rights to receive information. Citizenship arguments also conflict with market arguments because they stress the importance of equity. Starting from an assumption of equal human rights (whether civil, political or social, to use T. H. Marshall's distinction),[20] there is an inescapable drift towards some notion of equal rights of information and communication.

Like the ritual idea of television, a view that starts with citizenship carries many contradictions. Historically, the idea of citizenship has rarely been neutral, reflecting rather the often narrow interests of particular rising classes, and of emergent nation-states which had little time for members of competing communities. The heavy stress on participation can obscure the very legitimate reasons why people choose not to participate. There are also dangers in using a rhetoric of participation and democracy around a medium that has always been intrinsically top-down and manipulative. Apparently democratic arguments can easily be used to legitimize the struggles of one elite against another. There are also inescapable tensions between the localist ideology of community radio and television, emphasizing closeness to local experience, and an alternative that privileges the world of national parties, trade unions and associations. It is not obvious where the boundaries of the *civis* are to be found.

Both the ritual and the citizenship approaches lead to similar conclusions, the one starting from the needs of the community, the other from the rights of the individual. Television is good when it creates the conditions for people to participate actively in a community; when it provides them with the truest possible information; when it encourages membership and activity rather than passivity and alienation; and when it serves as an invigorator of the democratic process rather than as a medium for what Walter Lippman called the 'manufacture of consent'.

We can also take the argument beyond the political emphasis

of citizenship. Many would see other kinds of awareness as inherently good. Awareness of the pleasures and pains of others, of the world's social and economic structures, of science and religion, or of the means of enlightenment and spiritual maturity makes for a fuller realization of human potential. Others would ask of television whether it makes people better by offering role models, by suggesting ways of interacting with other people, or by providing narrative structures within which to make sense of life. In each case the quality of a particular programme, or of a television service, will depend entirely on its success in achieving these aims.

Arguments that start from the individual often suggest that television is useful not only as a means of receiving information or entertainment, but also as a means of expression. The traditional producer and consumer arguments assume that professionals (or the industry) will always provide services to passive audiences. The model is a top-down one. Others (starting perhaps from Bertolt Brecht's famous comments about radio becoming a means of communication) have suggested that broadcasting would be better organized as a set of channels with wide access to the means of production as well as reception. Writers as diverse as Hans Magnus Enzensberger and Alvin Toffler have written hopefully of a future when widespread interactivity is feasible, and when minorities have the same rights as majorities. Similar, often utopian, themes can be found in many writings about cable television and the wired society. Implicit in all of them is the idea that the act of creating and communicating is in some way superior to the act of receiving, so that television's 'true' quality is its capacity to offer widespread access.

These various attempts to link television to notions of the person all have a common theme: the link between information and action. They implicitly challenge one of the features of the television age, which is also an age of informational abundance. Much less than in the past is there any link between the information we receive and the actions we take. The vast majority of information which we receive from newspapers, billboards and cathode ray tubes is pure diversion, almost noise, an endless series of answers to unasked questions. By linking the qualities of television to the needs and virtues of active human beings, these various approaches suggest that the equation of more and worse may have a meaning that goes rather deeper than fears for tackier sets and more inarticulate scripts. The ultimate threat is that television will become just another heap of information, without any foundation in the experiences and needs of everyday life.

Each of these arguments is really about rootedness and relevance, and about the fear that television is their enemy. They are about the fear that television brings an end to any 'sense of place'.[21] But it is also possible to draw quite opposite conclusions from theories about human needs. Rather than being a link between information and action, television can be seen instead as one of many sources for creating stable structures of meaning, for resolving or working through problems. Seen in this light, television is at its best when it taps the subsconscious structures and archetypes with which people cope with life. Its highest qualities are realized not when it is rooted in a local culture or in uncovering information about the world, but rather when it is least rooted and most timeless. The universal themes of a programme like *Dallas*, a telenovella or even some pop videos, themes which can be used by people in almost any culture, are then of a higher quality, as television, than the lushest or most acute social drama.[22]

The Televisual Ecology

Television is often referred to as an ecology or eco-system. By this, people usually mean that it is a delicate and complex system that is not easily reducible to an economic description. It responds best to nurture and care rather than to brute force and mechanistic planning. Like an eco-system, it requires permanent adaptation, risk and experiment.

I want to use a wider sense of eco-system than this. Many commentators implicitly use ecological metaphors when they talk about television. They ask whether it is disruptive, polluting and corrupting, whether it promotes adaptation and evolution. Clearly, each of these metaphors is also an argument about quality. Better-quality broadcasting, like better-quality food or water, is non-polluting and non-corrupting: that is to say, it is broadcasting that does not introduce bad morals, hypocrisies or falsities, or that leaves the society better than it finds it.

The ecological analogy remains very influential. The popular belief that television contributes to violence and amorality, or to sexism and racism, is still strong, even though an enormous amount of research has failed to impute any direct effects. Ecological metaphors are attractive because television can feel like an alien invader, even in the cosy familiarity of the living room.

But their superficial appeal masks some unpleasant implications. For a start it must be agreed who is to say what is healthy and what is pathological. The suggestion that we need guardianship brings out the legitimate suspicion of any institution which takes it upon itself to distinguish what is healthy and what is not. A second problem is the inherent difficulty of agreeing about when it is justified to restrict free speech. The idea of protecting communities from televisual violence and pollution has become increasingly difficult to put into practice in a widely acceptable way.

Ideas of protection have been at their strongest in relation to children's television. There is wide agreement that children need to be protected from manipulative programmes, and from programmes that propagate 'bad' values. But even here, the ecological metaphor can be misleading. Thousands of years of folk tales and fairy stories have revealed both the boundlessness of children's imaginations and the apparent need for horror and morbidity to help make sense of the world. The argument could also be made more generally. It may be that a healthy society needs the invasion of alien, dangerous, subversive elements to maintain its moral and cultural integrity, and to learn about itself. Perhaps societies need to foster the vigour of their 'antibodies', through continual criticism and challenge, just as even the most reasonable argument requires constant criticism if it is to retain its sharpness. Perhaps the good and the bad depend on each other. The implication is that an overprotective and oversterilized television service will do no favours to the society of which it is part.

The one theme that can be salvaged from the ecological metaphors is the idea that truth needs to be protected from falsehood, and that television, like all the media, must play its part in sustaining truth and bearing witness. The argument is particularly pertinent in Britain in the 1990s, since it is most threatening to the two groups who now appear to have most power over broadcasting policy, the advertisers and politicians. These are the only two groups in Britain with exclusive rights of unedited access to the airwaves. They are also distinct from other broadcasters for two other reasons: both rely on emotive and irrational modes of argument to achieve their ends; and both broadcast information whose contents are closely bound up with their interests. This makes them distinct from the professional newreader or the teacher. In an important sense, it makes them stand against any ethos of truth telling.

This argument against manipulation and falsity does not have to depend on any final definitions of truth. It simply invokes the value of truth telling, and offers a small balance to the power of television. In other words, it suggests that the problem is not that television influences people (we simply do not know how much it does): the problem is that television *tries* to influence people.

Quality as Diversity

The most fundamental factor that makes it hard to sustain an ecological metaphor is the absence of a broad enough consensus about what is good or bad, healthy or unhealthy. The lack of centre in a society that contains everything from charismatic Christians to militant Muslims, radical feminists to xenophobic racists, helps to explain the crisis of the old forms of strong regulation that governed British broadcasting. It also gives us the seventh idea of quality, the idea of quality as diversity.

Most people express the view that a broadcasting system of high quality must offer a wide range of programmes. Much of the pleasure of television comes from moving between mass audience programmes and minority ones, from a comedy to a nature programme to a film. Diversity is built into the remit both of public service broadcasting generally (defined as a range of different programme types) and of Channel 4, which is charged with representing minority interests and a diversity (rather than a balance) of views.

The argument is also often made that a multicultural society composed of very different interests and experiences must be reflected in the media: diversity must be protected even when it conflicts with the imperatives of the market, of producer sovereignty, or of social solidarity. At a more philosophical level, there are many who would argue for diversity for its own sake as essential in a decentred world of multiple truths (or multiple fictions), where the centripetal force towards common perspectives and values must be resisted at all costs.

These varied arguments have something to be said for them, though they take us only so far. Diversity is rarely a good thing unless it is the right kind of diversity. The abstract idea of diversity leaves unanswered questions about how good or bad the diverse programmes or channels are: there is nothing obviously good about a diversity of truths and falsehoods, unless we believe that truths will always prevail over lies. There is also relatively little to be said for a system where minorities simply speak to themselves.

In recent years there has been a pervasive, and understandable, fear of privileging one type of communication over another. The general support for diversity, given force by the demands for access of those excluded from the medium, reflects this sensibility, which is so characteristic of the late twentieth century. But we now know some of the costs of this reluctance: crudely, it makes it harder to defend the good against the bad, the true against the false. The mood is now swinging back, not to where it was before, but to a more measured recognition of the need to achieve a balance in the organization of channels and broadcasting systems.

A more subtle understanding of diversity brings with it distinctions and even hierarchies with which to understand television as a medium. The rules appropriate for minority channels, perhaps for an ethnic minority with its own language, will be very different from those appropriate for a channel reaching twenty million viewers. The judgements and rules that apply to news or documentaries – the emphasis on truth telling and investigation – need not apply to light entertainment. The priorities for film and drama, which might place a greater emphasis on their aesthetic qualities, their ritual resonance or their ability to raise the awareness of the audience, would be different from those for sport or music.

Distinctions of this kind reflect the way people use television. Most people use television primarily for pleasure and relaxation. For much of the time it is a relatively low-involvement medium: it does not matter enormously what programmes are actually on or what they are saying. At other times television has quite different characteristics: the messages it conveys change people's lives, and the medium itself becomes present in large processes of change. The dangers arise when broadcasters lose sight of these differences: when 'the ratings' or 'the market' becomes the only criterion of judgement, or when television's 'metalanguage of entertainment' blunts broadcasters' commitment to truth, independence or social responsibility.

The Return to Quality

Much of the recent debate about quality has been one dimensional. Quality has been talked about as if it could be defined in a 'threshold' or 'hurdle', or, alternatively, as if it is a predictable effect of large programme production budgets. Neither is a satisfactory way of talking about a medium that is already well into middle age.

Some appreciation that television works on many different levels and in many different ways is a necessary condition for any meaningful discussion. Whether broadcasting is for entertainment, for enlightenment, for the creation of citizens or whole persons, for making profits, for sustaining the cultural capital of dominant classes, for uncovering the true natures of society and everyday life, or for preserving the morality and cohesion of the community makes all the difference. Each view of broadcasting's purpose brings with it a very different conception of quality. Each requires a different structure, a different set of relationships between programme makers, administrators and audiences.

The ideals of producer quality depend on creative autonomy and insulation from the pressures of ratings or political masters; the maximization of consumer satisfaction requires that viewers have a direct impact on programming decisions (whether through the 'market' and the remote control, or through using licence fee forms to allocate funds between channels). The quality of television as a medium depends on active criticism and on programme makers having the freedom to follow purely aesthetic criteria. The role of television as a medium of ritual and communion requires that priority is given to genuine mass channels, and to channels that serve clearly defined communities. The role of television as an enhancer of individuals depends on a strong awareness of its responsibilities as a forum, as an educator, as a teller of truths. All are legitimate purposes and all deserve a place in a broadcasting system that is adequate for a complicated modern society.

In facing up to this complex mix of values, rights and interests, those empowered to shape the medium need a degree of humility. One of the unsolicited lessons of recent broadcasting debates is that we still know remarkably little about how broadcasting functions, about its effects (or insignificance), about the nature of audiences, and about how television is really used. Today's arguments for radical change have to be seen for what they are: guesses, hopes, assertions and arguments by analogy rather than rigorous conclusions drawn from hard evidence and indisputable logic. They are not necessarily wrong, but no one should be surprised that the arguments are never concluded (or rather that it is history and not logic that decides the winners).

Faced with a period of rapid change, of new technologies, bids and conglomerations, the real challenge is to keep a sense of proportion and perspective, not only about the balance between change and conservation, but also about the balance between different interests and ideologies. When the weight of advertisers is growing, it is that much more important to stress the value of truth telling, disinterestedness and honesty; when the viewer is seen only as a consumer, it is that much more important to stress the viewer's position as a citizen, and, indeed, as someone who can contribute to making television as well as receiving it; when television is seen simply as throughput (a 'toaster with pictures'; as Mark Fowler put it), it becomes all the more important to show that it, too, can aspire to be an art; and when television is seen as just a mass of programmes bought and sold in an international market, it becomes all the more important to stress that a television service also plays an integral, even defining, role in the life and values of a community.

Notes

1 *Quality in Television, Programmes, Programme Makers, Systems*, Broadcasting Research Unit/John Libbey, London, 1989.
2 Gordon Hughes and David Vines, 'Regulation and strategic behaviour in commercial television', in *Deregulation and the Future of Commercial Television*, David Hume Institute, 1989, which focuses on what it describes as the 'upmarket Quality scenario'.
3 Peter Kellner, 'Like it or not: the audience speaks out', *Independent*, 17 November 1989.
4 David Morrison, *Invisible Citizens*, BRU/John Libbey, London, 1986.
5 op. cit. p. 14.
6 David Morley, *Family Television*, Comedia, London 1986.
7 Edward Buscombe, 'Creativity in television', *Screen*.
8 'The relationship of management with creative staff', Anthony Smith in the *Report of the Committee on the Future of Broadcasting*, Appendix I, HMSO, London, 1977, p. 140.
9 Mark Fowler and D. L. Brenner: 'A marketplace approach to broadcast regulation', *Texas Law Review*, 60, 1982.
10 Hence the arguments for preserving the licence fee expounded by Charles Jonscher in the HMSO report on *Subscription Television*, 1987.
11 Quoted in *Financial Times*, 22 September 1989.
12 George Akerloff, 'The market for "lemons": qualitative uncertainty and the market mechanisms', *Quarterly Journal of Economics*, August 1970.
13 Carl Shapiro, 'Premiums of high quality products as returns to reputation', *Quarterly Journal of Economics*, November 1983.
14 Neil Postman, *Amusing Ourselves to Death*, Penguin, Harmondsworth, 1986.

15 Horace Newcomb, *Television: the most popular art*, Anchor Doubleday, New York, 1974.

16 Umberto Eco, 'Innovation and repetition', in 'The moving image', *Daedelus*, fall 1985.

17 Pierre Bourdieu, *Distinctions*, Routledge and Kegan Paul, London, 1986.

18 James Carey, 'Communication and culture', *Communications Research*, summer 1975; also *Communication as Culture: essays on media and society*, Unwin Hyman, London, 1989.

19 Paddy Scannel, *The Communicative Ethos in Broadcasting*, ITSC, London, 1988.

20 T. H. Marshall, *Citizenship and Social Class*, Cambridge University Press, Cambridge, 1950.

21 See, for example, Joshua Meyrowitz, *No Sense of Place*, Oxford University Press, New York, 1986.

22 See, for example, Ien Ang, *Watching Dallas*, Routledge, London, 1993.

6

THE POWER OF THE WEAK

Soft and weak overcome hard and strong.

Tao Te Ching, 36

Engineering theory describes two types of control: strong power and weak power controls. Strong power controls use large quantities of energy relative to the processes they control, while weak power controls use very little. Most manual labour and most mechanical machines depend on strong power forms of control. The human brain, by contrast, is an example of a weak power control, using much less energy than the body it controls. Unlike the machinery of the Fordist production line, most of the machinery of post-Fordism uses weak power controls: the central processing unit of an automated factory, the chips that run a washing machine and the networks that control invoicing, warehouses or flows of accounting data all use much less energy, both physical and human, than the systems they replace. The weak power controls of post-Fordism also share one other characteristic with the human brain, their flexibility and adaptability: control can be quickly and easily reprogrammed through software. In this they reflect the essential properties of the computer, designed as the universal machine that could copy any other.

This essay argues that the replacement of strong power by weak power controls in the physical machinery of post-Fordism is being matched by a parallel transformation of social organization and control, a transformation that is also one from strong to weak types of control, or at any rate a shift in the balance between the strong and weak, the soft and hard forms of control which must coexist in any organization or society.

The relevance of this discussion is that, in any deep structural shift, new opportunities and challenges are thrown up for social actors: political parties, government departments, firms and individuals seeking to shape their lives in the interstices left by formal organizations. Those that go with the grain of change, adapting it to their fundamental values, can direct their energies to growth. Those that resist, locked into the modes of thought and organizations of passing eras, become impotent and ill at ease with their times.

At the close of the twentieth century few have fully escaped the profound impact of the various models lumped together in the word 'Fordism'. Fordism was in many ways the apotheosis of faith in structure and strong power control. Within its organizations authority derives from position rather than from knowledge or ability. Formal rules determine how decisions are to be made and responsibility allocated. Structured as a pyramid, the organization depends on vertical lines of authority and accountability. Control absorbs a lot of time and energy. Most communication is vertical, between superiors and subordinates, rather than horizontal. It is built around the bureaucracy, which developed in its modern form in the nineteenth century and was modelled on armies' strong power command-and-control structure. As anyone who has worked in a large bureaucracy knows, most of its energy is used simply reproducing itself. The same is true of the classic modern corporation, dictatorial, hierarchical and bound by a rigid division of labour. Both aim to bring predictability and order to a chaotic world. As a result, neither leaves much scope for initiative, imagination or autonomy.

The weak power structures of the new times are very different. They tend to be decentralized, without a single point of leadership; communication is horizontal; structures are cellular rather than pyramid-like, a shifting mosaic rather than the kind of structure that can be drawn as a diagram. The units and cells tend to regulate themselves, rather than being governed by rules and commands that flow downwards. Accountability can flow in more than one direction at once. Where the strong power structure is concerned with predictability, the best weak power structures thrive on fluidity, change and the creative use of chaos. Above all, energies are directed outwards rather than inwards to sustaining and reproducing a fixed structure.

The distinction between the strong power systems of Fordism and weak power structures of the new times has obvious implications for the socialist project at the end of the century. Like most of the really compelling utopian visions, Marx's communism was a vision of great autonomy, in which the individual's creative control over his or her own life is reconciled with the common needs of the community. In theory the state was to wither away, to be concerned only with the 'administration of things', a light layer of co-ordination over an organic, self-regulating society. In practice, however, socialism has been associated with strong power structures – with the bureaucratic public institution, the central plan, the hierarchical trade union and party, organized as layer upon layer of committees and officials – structures that leave almost as little scope for autonomous control as the Fordist corporation. Democracy in socialist traditions has also usually been conceived in terms of pyramid-like, vertically layered structures. Moreover, what we are brought up to see as the highest form of politics, the face-to-face meeting, the direct democratic control of the Athenian agora or the branch meeting is also a strong power structure, using prodigious amounts of time and energy relative to the things that are the subjects of its decisions. This is why periods of intense politicization tend to be short, why pure democracies often degenerate into control by self-appointed cliques, and why Oscar Wilde said that socialism would never come because there are not enough evenings in the week.

Though weak power structures have a long history in socialist thought, in co-operatives, mutual aid organizations and guilds, and more recently in the traditions of 1968 and the new movements, it is on the leading edges of capitalism that they are now developing most quickly. During the recession of the late 1970s and early 1980s, many transnational corporations found themselves too unwieldy and inflexible for the environment in which they had to work. The failings of Ford's global car strategy, an attempt to create worldwide strong power structures around common designs, are well known. The economic pressures of intensified competition, of a more internationalized and volatile economy, protected by fewer regulations and barriers, engendered a forced march of organizational experiment in search of the elusive key to sustainable competitiveness. The intellectual labour of a small army of management consultants, business schools, think-tanks, theorists and corporate strategists was mobilized to answer the question of how structures could be re-ordered to improve productivity and efficiency.

The result has been a widespread conversion to the virtues of more flexible, weak power structures. Central to this view is a sense of the growing importance of creativity and knowledge in advanced economies: in new sectors such as biotechnology or artificial intelligence, knowledge, creativity and imagination become as important to economic success as narrowly conceived efficiency. The organizational problem is to mobilize people's commitment and mental powers rather than to exploit them more intensively. Though pyramidal bureaucracies are very good at implementing a given set of rules, they are strikingly ill-suited to creation and innovation, discouraging the kinds of risk and radical thought that produce the most lucrative values in a knowledge-based economy.

Traditions of cultural production offer more suitable models: artists are left to themselves because they produce better art that way. The same is true of the inventor or designer. Their managers and paymasters can only have a limited understanding of what they do and must leave to them the job of organizing their own work. Rather than issuing a stream of commands like the army general or the manager of a traditional factory, managers become more like the conductor of an orchestra, or the publishing editor, a co-ordinator of groups with specialized skills. A degree of control is ceded so as to improve the quality of what is produced. Looser structures of this kind work better at encouraging risk and innovation and at spreading knowledge. The pre-eminent centres of high-technology production such as Silicon Valley and Route 128 around Boston operate like networks, linking groups of inventors, entrepreneurs, academics and investors, in a form of industrial district that is quite distinct from the Detroit of

General Motors or Ford, or the classic corporations that producd steel, chemicals or ships. Even IBM, still the dominant corporation in the information industry and a famously 'tight' organization, has experimented by creating weak power network structures within itself, with quasi-independent units in fields such as medical instruments and robotics: the aim is to emulate something of the hot-house looseness of Silicon Valley while maintaining tight central oversight.

Though weak power structures are most apparent in leading-edge sectors, they are also spreading throughout the economy as all firms take on some of the characteristics of knowledge producers. Around half the value of a car or aeroplane is accounted for by electronics and computers. The design of a product, even a piece of furniture or clothing, is an informational task, and the quality of this design has come to be seen as a more important source of competitive advantage than low costs of production. This emphasis on the informational content of products is reflected in organizational structures. Many large firms, both in the advanced sectors and more generally, are taking on the character of networks of independent units, often organized as profit centres, able to choose whether to co-operate with other units of the same firm and able to take their own initiatives. There is also more collaboration across company boundaries whether in the form of the joint venture, the licensing agreement or the intercorporate network linking suppliers and distributors. Small firms are moving in a similar direction, organizing loose federations, marketing and research co-operatives, or joint training projects, often in collaboration with local government and academic institutions. Communication in all directions is both more intensive and extensive, a sometimes confusing mix of competition and co-operation.

The strong power structures of Fordism were held together by discipline and the contract. In the Faustian compacts of Ford and Taylor the worker traded autonomy for the wage packet; in the factory every task was specified in detail, every deviation punished. The same was true of relationships with other firms, where contracts sought to cover any possible outcome and where price competition acted as a ruthless discipline. Within weak power structures there are very different kinds of bond. Within the firm, ethos, self-esteem and peer pressure are emphasized. Corporate ideology takes on a new significance, demanding loyalty and devotion from the worker, so that discipline is internalized within the worker's own conscience. It is no coincidence that investment in corporate television has in recent years come to match investment in the communications networks used to oversee flows of goods and money. Soft control has become as important as hard control.

Within networks of firms the experience of working together and the accumulation of trust come to replace explicit controls. Long-term relationships become more important than short-term profit. This is the essence of the successful joint venture or industrial district: companies learn to co-operate, to share ideas and contracts. Designers, researchers and inventors meet and argue in cafés, pubs and restaurants, creating a milieu of social creativity from which all benefit. Universities, source of the raw materials of the knowledge industries, become 'like the corner café where artisans solve one another's problems and share – or steal – one another's ideas'. Sociability has taken on an economic value in the era of post-Fordism, something recognized by the many governments trying to create synthetically sociable environments to foster science and innovation in such diverse places as Phoenix Arizona, Sophia Antipolis in southern France, Novo-Sibirsk in Russia and Kyushu in Japan. Japan's ambitious Technopolis project, aimed at creating futuristic knowledge cities under the aegis of academia, industry and local government, is probably the purest example of this.

A similar pattern can be seen in the plethora of new, semi-public bodies springing up around computing, once thought of as the most chronically entrepreneurial and competitive of all industries: Sematech, MCC and COS in the USA, Esprit, Alvey and JESSI in Europe, are all semi-public programmes and institutions within which companies learn to co-operate and compete at the same time.

These practices are reflected in theory. The dominant business theories of the late 1980s, popularized in the writings of John Naisbitt, Peters and Waterman, Rosabeth Moss Kantor and Sho-

shanna Zuboff, are awash with ideas that seem like pale echoes
of 1968 (and indeed the 1840s), stressing the virtues of relative
equality, network forms, creativity, the abolition of hierarchy,
and the definition of work as play. It is easy to be cynical about
capitalism's ability to co-opt the counter-culture, and it is certainly
true that these ideas often play the role of ideology in its pure
sense, systematic distortions that mask the real play of power.
But it would be quite wrong to ignore the basic insights they
offer. Most important perhaps is the sense that the authoritarian,
vertical corporation is beginning to outlive its usefulness: dictatorial organizational may still work in assembly plants and super-
markets, but it is inefficient in research and development or in
the production of such things as semiconductors and cars. If
people are treated like things they will behave like things, unwilling to care about what they produce, or to use their intelligence
to solve the problems that inevitably arise. This is one of the
striking features of the experience of automation. Automation
seemed to offer the ultimate form of Fordism, an electronic
guarantee of total control from the top. Instead it has turned
out to depend on highly motivated, highly skilled workers able
continually to reprogram machines; computer aided design,
manufacture and engineering cannot be imposed from on top but
rather depend on the permanent collaboration of teams working
on design, production engineering and production itself.

These experiences of automation point to the second factor
underlying the move towards weak power structures: the properties of new communications technologies. These properties are
not as straightforward as they at first seem. In principle any
communication technology can be used to tighten centralized
control. The telephone strengthened the central office, while the
computer network allows it instantly to monitor sales in shops
or the output of factories. The Polish economist Oskar Lange
believed that the computer could solve all the problems of socialist
central planning, monitoring every detail of economic activity at
the centre so as perfectly to match supply and demand. In practice,
however, technology runs up against the context in which information is produced. Within pyramidal structures those lower
down usually have good reason to distort the information they

give to their superiors, an experience common to East European central planning and Western multinationals. Manipulating information to magnify successes, hide failures or bid for resources is about the only means available for negotiating control with superiors.

Communications technologies have a paradoxical effect in this respect: their potential cannot be realized unless people have an incentive to provide good information (on the GIGO, garbage in, garbage out, principle). As a result, even when brought in to centralize control they often turn out to bring a devolution of power and responsibility in their wake. This points to a more general feature of the post-Fordist economy: each investment in communications technology brings a reappraisal of how control is organized. The inherent flexibility of computerized systems means that the revolution in the means of production described by Marx has been joined by a permanent revolution in techniques of control. Change and flux come to be accepted as normal rather than being seen as destabilizing threats, while structures come to be seen as inherently malleable.

Communications technologies can also be used to undermine strong power pyramids more directly. Within a few years of its invention it was recognized that the telephone could subvert hierarchies, making it possible for the chief executive to speak directly to the foreman. As networks carry more information, not just conversations but also data about accounts, patents and market research findings, pyramid structures dissolve from within. The traditional role of middle management was that of a relayer of commands and information. Commands were relayed downwards, while information about what was happening on the shop floor or in the office was relayed upwards in the form of written reports. With advanced networks, the LANs (local area networks) and private ISDNs (integrated services digital networks), these functions become redundant: specialized units can communicate horizontally, overseen by much slimmer top managements which themselves have instant access to data from the shop floor. Decisions can be decentralized precisely because central oversight is easier; once decentralized their quality often improves because they are made by people familiar with the complexities of the situation. Again, good control depends on knowing when it needs to be loosened. This is not a new insight. In the eighteenth century the Empress Maria Theresa even awarded a special medal to officers who turned the tide in battle by disobeying orders, an unusual example of an autocrat encouraging insubordination.

Weak and Strong Power in Politics

The combined effect of new technologies and new attitudes has yet to have anything like the same impact on other areas of social life: political parties and voluntary organizations are only just beginning to think about how the networking of computers allows them to rethink their organizational structures. But the more general move to weak power structures is already apparent. Awareness of the economic inefficiency of strong power structures is matched by a growing awareness of their inefficiency in politics. Where the economic organization is concerned with productivity and profit, the effective political organization is the one that can respond to its constituency, successfully articulating alternatives and mobilizing energies for campaigns. It is the inability of political parties, unions and single-issue movements to be efficient in this sense that has prompted a new interest in more flexible weak power structures. Many of these echo older models: the corresponding societies of eighteenth-century Britain, radical religious movements, co-operative and mutual aid organizations were often organized as what we would now call networks, polycephalous or many-headed, without fixed rules, bound together horizontally by common beliefs. Weak power structures have also often coexisted with strong power ones, albeit uneasily: the shop stewards movement with the trade-union bureaucracy, the guerrilla cells with the party in exile. Over the last fifty years, however, it has been the strong power structures that have generally predominated: Fordism in the economy was precisely replicated by the most successful social-democratic and communist parties.

The era of strong power political institutions may now be coming to an end, at least in the advanced industrialized countries.

Their weaknesses have long been apparent. Like the Fordist corporation, the 'Fordist' parties have proved ill-equipped to exploit the opportunities offered by crisis and chaos. On both left and right the parties have become the rather sluggish mediums for change and new ideas rather than their instigators. In the 1990s, more than ever, it is the weak power structures that seem most in tune with the times, the most creative and the most effective at mobilizing new energies. Obvious examples include the women's and environmental movements which have usually been organized as horizontal networks, without the need for a single programme, a single leadership, a hierarchy of officials and committees. Instead communication is horizontal, a continually negotiated relationship between autonomous groups bound together by shared ideas and values rather than a single structure. The same is true of the new right: the ideas and programmes of Thatcherism and Reaganism were generated not within political parties but by a loose web of think-tanks, writers, executives and politicians, a weak power network, often in considerable tension with the formal structures of party and civil service.

In some countries technology is beginning to assist in the move to weak power structures. On a videotex network like Minitel in France or Compuserve in the USA, activists can very quickly link together on a campaign, sharing ideas, research and best practices without the need to meet together or establish a formal institution with committees, standing orders and officials: the 'virtual' campaign comes to stand alongside the 'virtual' classroom and the 'virtual' laboratory, existing in electronic space rather than the formal, physical space of meetings and conferences, its structures instantly formed or dissolved.

The one area where weak power structures have yet to make a major impact is in the organization of the state. Governments remain quintessentially strong power structures, devising policies and programmes at the top and passing them down through a hierarchical bureaucracy to people at the bottom. Governments' inefficiencies as control systems have been recognized for a long time: their basic failing, probably most effectively described by Friedrich Hayek, is their inefficiency as information systems. The minister or permanent secretary is meant both to represent the public and to control a vast bureaucracy. Both are inherently impossible tasks. No one can realistically represent the interests of fifty-five million different people. Equally, no one can really know what is happening in each section of a nationalized industry, each social security office or hospital ward. The solution governments adopt is to simplify in order to control: the form, the account and the statistic are all ways of coping with an overcomplicated world, and are of course the very lifeblood of a bureaucracy. To borrow a term from computing, the state preprocesses: it simplifies the information it gathers in order to make it easier to process.

This characteristic of government colours any attempt at public or democratic control. The public control that is exercised through the Morrisonian corporation and the Stalinist bureaucracy is channelled through the summit of a pyramid (the minister), and is then passed downwards through the apparatus of the state. The public's interests and aspirations are passed all the way up the pyramid and then all the way down. Like the strong power corporation, this approach worked fairly well at providing standardized solutions, such as standard housing, large-scale industrial manufacture, or standardized benefits. But as societies become more differentiated, with very different needs and interests, an interdependent web of specialist groups, the flaws of the strong power state become more apparent. Like the strong power corporation, it is better at treating people like things, in one dimension: it deals with quantifiable indicators so that in the case of housing, for example, it uses a points system rather than qualitative indicators such as a preference for a high or low position, a style or type of neighbourhood. Faced by complexity, the state responds with simplicity.

This critique of the state long predates the age of post-Fordism. However, it takes on much greater weight now because it is essentially an argument about complexity. The more complex a structure is, the harder it is to exercise top-down control, and complexity is at the heart of the new times of post-Fordism, of less standardized products, a more complicated division of labour and more differentiated cultures and identities. In a more complicated, interdependent system, the traditional socialist programme for radically simplifying society, and replacing the convoluted structures of entrenched powers with a unified programme, becomes less effective. The solution, parodied by Brecht as that of 'dissolving the people and electing another', becomes too costly as the state is unable singlehandedly to replicate the complex social ecologies of advanced systems of health, education or agriculture.

The failings of the strong power, standardizing state have become one of the right's trump cards. The right's informational critique of the state, given its most coherent form by Hayek in the 1940s, argued for the virtues of the market as an information system. The ideal market could be seen as a decentralized processing system, a weak power structure instantly responding to the changing needs of consumers, by contrast with the simplifying, standardizing and remote state. The market could even be seen as more democratic than the formal institutions of democracy: in the market everyone at least exerts influence, whereas in the democracy the choices of up to two-thirds of the population may be completely ignored. The democratic election offers at best a handful of choices, while the market, at least in theory, offers an almost infinite array of choices for those with the money to exercise it.

At a time when the market was mainly producing very standardized products using highly centralized decision-making structures. Hayek's argument was only partially convincing. Forty years later, when capitalism has learnt much more quickly than the state the virtues of flexible specialization, differentiation and more subtle, multidimensional market research techniques, the critique becomes devastating. In contrast to the strong power structures of public control, the private control of the sovereign consumer can be portrayed as real, visible and tangible.

Forms of Control

This promise of control was central to the right's success in setting the political agendas of the 1980s: control was promised not only at the individual level, through owning your own house or determining your children's education, but also in terms of influence over larger institutions. For a customer or shareholder of British Telecom or British Gas, control can be portrayed as concrete ('we answer to you'), where the control exercised through Parliament and ministers was abstract and remote. But though the right has articulated a clear vision of control that is human in scale and accessible to the majority, it is a vision that is only partially formed. The right has found it hard to develop a coherent position on control over one's own body (through food, health or reproductive choice), or on control over one's own work; moreover, control is seen as something that can be exercised only by the individual, rather than by the small group or the community.

Faced by the right's assault on the strong power state, the left has generally answered with a call for more democracy. Democracy is seen as the way to give people control over their own lives, the solution to the remoteness and unresponsiveness of public services. Real democratic structures, however, can be as unsatisfactory as strong power states and one-dimensional markets. Some of their flaws have already been touched on: the dictatorship of the majority, the tendency for the demands of the structure to override a concern for the quality and contents of decisions. An equally important flaw derives from the nature of control. Real control is never costless but requires investment of time and resources. The control of the consumer depends on finding out what alternatives are available, about the real qualities of what is being bought. The control of the voter, or of someone who sits on committees, is equally dependent on time invested in finding out about alternatives, about how to implement them, about what representatives and officials are really doing. An understanding of the connection between knowledge and real political control was central to the nineteenth-century workers' libraries and educational movements: the connection between time and participation has also formed part of the feminist critique of the labour movement's cult of meeting-going machismo.

The simple fact is that our ability to exercise control is strictly limited by time. Most people intuitively understand this, and happily leave jobs to others. One of the virtues of complex societies is that we do not actually need to understand how a VCR works or how municipal rubbish collection is organized. We do not control every aspect of life because if we did there would be no time for work, love and play. The fully democratized society in which we had to take part in all decisions is for many a vision of hell, an endless branch or committee meeting writ horribly large. Because most people limit the time they devote to participating in democratic structures, control always threatens to fall on to self-appointed cliques who effectively disenfranchise those unable or unwilling to participate. As a result, democratic structures that demand intensive participation often prove unstable. This has been the experience of many collectives and co-operatives, where the principled commitment to full participation in decisions results in ever more time being spent in meetings, and, in the worst cases, a sense that people are interfering in each other's work.

It should be stressed that these are not arguments against democracy, but rather arguments against the idea that democracy is any more a universal panacea than the market. Both give the individual some control, but both also limit the scope of this control, and tend to become distorted. Any convincing vision of a future society must recognize the need for multiple structures of control: the coexistence of representative and direct democracy, rights of removal or veto, market-type controls and the control that is exercised through ethos and moral suasion. A convincing view of change also needs to reflect such a pluralism of structure.

Th manifestos and programmes of the left have usually asked how control can be exercised over society; they search for the commanding heights, the alternative sources of power that need to be neutralized. In societies more dependent on weak power structures this approach loses its purchase: rather than being concentrated in clearly identifiable centres, power becomes systemic in nature, less respectful of boundaries whether geographical or sectoral. Where there are fewer pyramids, control can no longer be exercised through appointing a few new chief executives. Change can no longer be conceived as something that can be imposed by a government seen as outside society, nor as something that can be achieved through imposing a structure, whether democratic or technocratic, on to society; instead lasting change must be seen as organic and endogenous, harder to achieve but harder to reverse.

Escaping from what could be called the vertical view of change is essential to understanding the promise of weak power structures. The promise is of a very different kind of state that does not seek to control society directly, but rather sets the parameters within which society controls itself, such as rights and obligations, and rules on buildings or pollution emissions. Such a state, acting as an enabler and a catalyst, engaged in permanent dialogue with specialist groups, trade unions, banks and community organizations, would begin to take on some of the character of weak power systems. This is not to say that it would be enfeebled, but rather that it would be aware of the limits of effective control. The outlines of such an approach are already visible. One example is in the regulation of industry. Deregulation of industries was meant to bring the removal of state controls and their replacement by the market. Instead, in industries like air, telecommunications and trucking, regulations have often had to become stricter as competition has been introduced and protections eroded, so as to prevent tendencies towards monopoly. What has changed has been the nature of control. Where in the past governments could lay down operational guidelines, and could seek to run an airline or telephone company, today their rules concern the parameters of operation, the rules for access and interconnection of networks, the setting of technical standards or maximum prices that can be charged. In a more complex environment top-down control becomes ineffective: instead the state becomes an overseer, a regulator of independent and competing organizations. This does not mean that control becomes less effective. In the case of telephones, for example, it may be easier to lay down targets and penalties to encourage British Telecom and its competitors to provide cheap services for those on low incomes than it is to initiate and implement such a programme downwards through the public bureaucracy.

This example shows how public controls can interweave with the discipline of markets. It also illuminates the limits of the right's thinking. For the right the problems of restructuring the state are relatively simple. Across the board the market must be allowed to penetrate and replace administrative structures. Regulations must be swept away. On the demand side the individual consumer must be allowed to exercise choice, while in supply, subcontracting and privatization use the discipline of the market to achieve efficiency. This fetishization of the market reveals the right's only partial understanding of weak power structures. In the right's vision of the reconstructed state, control is exercised only through price and profit: though they have been pioneered in the leading sectors of capitalism, none of the soft controls and loose structures of post-Fordism have yet to make an impact on the right's theory of how the world works.

Real markets combine many types of control and communication. Price works alongside trust, flows of inside information and shared knowledge, authority and ethos. The same would be true of the weak power post-Fordist state. Wherever possible small groups would become responsible for their own day-to-day decisions, as is already happening in education, health and social services. These would be able to form networks, share resources and collaborate. Accountability would be restructured so that it flowed in several directions at once, simultaneously to funding bodies, workers and users.

There are concrete examples of this happening already: housing associations co-operating on public housing projects, accountable simultaneously to their members, to the state and to prospective customers/members; another example is the Bologna law that requires developers to gain the support of local people as well as planning authorities so that they are disciplined simultaneously by the market and by two parallel democratic structures. Other possible examples might include publicly-funded old people's homes where managements are also accountable to those they look after; independent networks of midwives or acupuncture specialists providing services to NHS patients and regulating their own training and standards; credit unions (independent community organizations offering cheap loans) evolving out of estates to co-operate with municipal town card credit schemes of the kind beginning to emerge around the country; competing publicly funded development or training agencies, each with a distinct identity and ethos, and each developing its own networks and constituency among firms and workers; and the simultaneous use of parent/pupil election of school governors with voucher systems to allow for choice between schools. Each example recognizes the need for multiple structures of accountability that allow the citizen to exercise control simultaneously as a voter, a customer and a participant.

Every society has to strike a balance between the soft and the hard forms of control, between freedom and discipline. A society without any hard controls, any strict and impersonal rules, will tend to descend into corruption, clientilism and prejudice. But a society with too many will simply stagnate. The great excitement of our times is that the combination of far greater flexibility in technology and a still spreading democratic culture means that there is more room for imagination and innovation in the ways things are done, the ways in which internal autonomy is combined with external discipline, than ever before. Lenin's view that there was no alternative to Taylorism in production, that each mode of production entailed a fixed set of organizational solutions, now looks to have been very much a product of its time rather than a universal principle.

The move from strong to weak power forms of control, though still fragmented and uncertain, still resisted by those in all areas who cling to more heavy-handed forms of control, is an epochal shift. It is a necessary and unavoidable response to more complex societies that are increasingly dependent on knowledge, creativity and communication for their economic survival. It is a shift that socialist and radical movements and parties ignore at their peril.

In principle the virtues of weak power structures should be immediately evident to socialists; they resonate with the best traditions of self-definition and activity, the radical response to the impositions of capitalism and governments. But tradition dies hard, as does the attachment to formal, vertical structures. As time passes, the costs of this attachment will grow, manifested as political failure, frustration and disillusion; as is the nature of strong power structures, energies will be absorbed internally rather than directed outwards. Against the odds capitalism will have successfully defined a radical set of ideas to its own ends.

If, however, the left does learn to experiment with weak power structures, with the organizational forms that are most in tune with the times, it will become clear that the crisis of socialism is more a crisis of structures than one of values. Moreover, it will be harder to doubt that, just as the moral and philosophical roots of socialism, the belief in co-operation, compassion and responsibility, in values that transcend the narrowly material, all far predate the historical forms of socialism, so will they also outlast them.

7

THE REIMAGINATION OF
THE PUBLIC SECTOR

A revolution is under way in thinking about government. The technicalities of administrative tinkering that dominated the debates of earlier decades have been swept aside in a reappraisal of everything governments do. Their agencies are no longer deemed innocent until proven guilty or seen as essentially benign instruments of the public interest. Instead, a set of institutions that had come to seem a natural part of modern societies have found themselves open to a persistent challenge, charged with costing too much, with inflexibility and with neglect of the citizens they were meant to serve.

For a time it looked as if the public sectors might indeed be swept away in a libertarian revolution of the market, with government cut back to the core public goods of security and law enforcement. Instead much of the world faces an impasse. On the one hand, the divine rights which at one point states seemed to be accruing are unlikely ever to return. Modernity's erosion of deference and certainty has hit the state. On the other hand, no one has yet offered very credible alternatives to the nation-state's monopoly of power, its role as solver of last resort, and as guarantor of security whether social, economic or physical. Even as nation-states wane, they face a remarkable absence of serious competitors, and wherever people congregate together they tend to see a wide range of goods and services as inherently public.

This essay sets out how the impasse may be solved, partly through a harder-headed analysis of the definition of public goods, and partly through a rethink of the ethics, accountability and organization of public bodies. As we shall see, the hardest theoretical task has been to define the appropriate boundaries of the public sector, whether as owner, regulator or strategist. But the more immediate tasks have all been about coping with economics, and it is these concerns which continue to drive the reform process: in particular, the interaction of a remorseless rise in the cost of providing services and steadily growing demands, and the fundamental imbalance between a public economy characterized by stagnant productivity and a private economy characterized by steady progress in technologies and productivity.

On the supply side of the public economy, costs increase steadily because it is impossible to force productivity up in such labour-intensive activities as cleaning, teaching and counselling. Since productivity is increasing in manufacturing industry and services like banking, the relative cost of public services tends to rise: a phenomenon described by the American economist William Baumol as a cost disease. Where technology is applied, as in high-tech medicine, it only rarely replaces labour. Often better supply – such as the ability to treat new ailments – simply increases demand. Those applications of technology which could dramatically increase productivity – such as the extension of Open University practices to normal university education, the use of electronic tagging or the automation of benefits – are either in their infancy or fiercely resisted for the obvious reason that they threaten jobs.

The result of the productivity barrier is that costs rise remorselessly. In the UK education spending rose by an average 0.4 per cent per year in the 1980s while standards were widely felt to be falling; health economists reckon that across the OECD, medical services require real funding increases of 1.5 per cent[1] a year simply to keep services constant. At the same time, demand is on an upward gradient with the familiar pressure of an ageing population and rising expectations in health and education, exacerbated by growing demands for training or environmental

improvement. In Britain, the population over eighty-five is
expected to rise from 0.8 million in 1987 to 1.4 million in 2025.
The elderly, who already account for half of all social security
spending, will rise in numbers by around 1 per cent each year.
The cost of the basic state pension will rise by 52 per cent in
real terms by 2030.

This scissors effect of supply and demand has also been wors-
ened by the peculiar structures of public finance. In Britain local
finance – through the rates and briefly the poll tax – has not
grown with GDP in the way that income, VAT and corporation
tax do. In other countries, too, local services tend to depend on
less secure fiscal foundations than those run from the centre. As
a result, there has been a perpetual upwards pressure on tax
rates, and thus a perpetual source of political controversy around
the level of public spending. Such political controversy has also
been exacerbated by the failure of tax systems to make the transition from the mass taxes of mid-century to more focused, specialized taxes. Too often taxes have remained opaque and blunt,
without any clear connection between what is raised and what
is spent, without any of the rights which consumers expect, and
without the transparency which modern societies value.

But if economics has been the prime cause of crisis, it is not
the only one. The crisis is also one of purpose, as goals such as
poverty relief, microeconomic efficiency, social integration and
the protection of habitual living standards clash. The result is
that, broadly speaking, there are now at least six contending
explanations of what the public sector is for.

One is the traditional idea of the 'residual' welfare system as
the safety net for the poor governed by income testing. This idea
remains in its purest forms in US systems such as Medicaid, and
has its roots in the alms-giving traditions of many cultures and
the poor relief systems, one of the most important of which took
form in the English Poor Law Act of 1601, subsequently the
model for the USA and much of the Commonwealth.

A second view is William Beveridge's model of the welfare
state as a universal system of social insurance for risks, such as
unemployment or sickness, that are 'so general and uniform' that
they should be a collective responsibility, with uniform benefits

to remove stigma combined with a system of contributions that keeps the system comprehensible. Similar ideas inform many of the continental systems, often rooted in Catholic social thinking.

A third, related view sees much of the public sector as a set of more narrowly conceived insurance mechanisms, many of them mimicking private insurance systems, with distribution more closely linked to contribution than to need, and justifiable only because of failure in insurance markets.

A fourth is the left's view of the public sector as a fully fledged system of redistribution and social engineering, parallel to fiscal redistribution through the tax and benefits system, combined with remnants of the belief that the practices of the sector prefigure a future socialist society.

A fifth view, rapidly becoming the most influential of all, sees the public sector as nothing more than a set of service agencies, in principle indistinguishable from private companies.

And a sixth is a libertarian argument for doing away with the public sector wherever it provides essentially private goods such as pensions or health, and replacing it with market provision, so that, given a socially acceptable redistribution of wealth, people can buy their own education and health in the marketplace, or for that matter choose to spend money on foreign holidays and beer.

These models coexist in many different combinations: Canada, for example, combines European-style tax funding of medical care with largely private provision; Germany combines social insurance with a private medical system. All six conceptions can coexist within a single system, as they have done in the various parts of the British public sector that have been subjected to the conflicting pressures of radical right-wing national government and radical left-wing local authorities.

The consequence has been a pervasive ideological confusion, aggravated by the absence of clear principles defining the boundaries of public and private, state and market. Part of the reason is that in any modern society they are inextricably bound up with each other. But there are also deeper reasons. The extension of the state beyond its traditional role as holder of the monopoly of violence, upholder of law and defender of the value of money is a remarkably recent phenomenon. The state as we understand it is a creation of the last 150 years. In Britain the state bureaucracy tripled between 1891 and 1911. In the USA the federal bureaucracy grew from 600 in 1831 to 13,000 fifty years later. Since then there have been successive waves of rapid expansion. In the EC, for example, in the twenty years between 1967 and 1986 public spending as a proportion of GDP rose from 36.4 to 48.3 per cent. These rapid growths appear to have developed faster than any deep-rooted public acceptance of the boundaries of the state, particularly in its relation to the family.

There are also profound cultural factors at work. Popular attitudes as to what is the proper domain of public and private are in continual flux. To take just one example, in medieval times the cure of souls was a public responsibility for the church, the cure of bodies a private responsibility for the individual. Today these roles are reversed. In fifty years' time the individual's psychic condition may again become a public concern, their physical condition much more a private responsibility in an era of fatal sexually transmitted diseases and heightened awareness of the importance of lifestyle.

A third reason is that economics has proved no better at defining what the boundaries of the public sector should be. There is wide, though not universal, agreement that the state should control the provision of classic public goods – those which are inherently hard to commoditize because use by one person does not reduce what is available for others – such as roads, clean air, science and defence. But since the state has expanded to provide goods according to right, such as health and education, and to produce goods such as energy, water and waste removal where individual charges roughly cover costs, the argument has become much more complex. Many of these goods and services can be, and often are, provided within a market. Yet most combine the characteristics of both public and private goods: health, for example, is never a purely private matter; nor is the level of other people's schooling or their transport choices.

Financial Control

These uncertainties have kept the intellectual debate at a high pitch. But it has been the economic crisis which has driven the process of reform and which has forced reorganization, primarily to cut costs but also to improve quality. Britain is not unusual in that its civil service restructuring followed a financial management initiative, rather than a human resource initiative or a quality of service initiative. The need to contain public spending drove both the long-term structural reforms and the short-term measures of containment – cutting the quality of service, sweating labour (albeit at the cost of undermining the quality of the workforce) and shifting provision out into the domestic sphere.

But these reforms have been just part of a much larger story of restructuring throughout the world. Although the changes have been most rapid in the Anglo-Saxon countries, perhaps because of the relative weakness of state traditions, many of the same symptoms of crisis and many of the same debates are now raging in other countries. Out of them have emerged a set of common policy responses to the economic crisis.

1   The most common have been measures to raise funds for the state. These have included privatizations and user charges – tolls for roads, top-up tuition fees, prescription charges – and the move from universal benefits, such as the flat-rate component of pensions in Sweden, New Zealand or Canada, to targeted benefits. As well as releasing funds for other uses, these have also been justified on grounds of social equity, since the middle classes are often the main beneficiaries of public services. According to the OECD, for example, in virtually all its member countries 'high income groups are far and away the largest beneficiaries of government spending on education'.[2] In many countries, rigorous analysis soon shows that public sectors (and the accumulated paraphernalia of tax concessions) work as often to redistribute resources towards the rich as they do to the poor.

2   A second set of reforms has been designed to tighten financial control within the context of public funding. The contracting out of services, initially those like refuse collection and catering,

more recently others like community care or wheel clamping, has been part of a process of replacing bureaucratic control by the stricter discipline of contractual relationships between different layers of the state, and between the state and private firms, and by the disciplines provided by managed internal markets. The same motive has driven the trend towards greater internal transparency. The use of management information systems, performance indicators (however crude) and more rigorous accounting systems has been intended to force greater clarity about the opportunity cost of decisions (that is, the cost in terms of forgone alternatives). Nowhere is this more apparent than in the National Health Service, where doctors have been turned into utilitarian philosophers and financial planners, required to weigh up the relative virtues of dialysis and hip replacements.

3   The third set of policies of reform has involved a separation of the determination of ends from the means of implementation. In Britain this has taken various forms: in the purchaser–provider split in health care which is now being copied in a number of other countries; and in the Executive Agencies, quasi-independent public bodies working on contract from central government, which have radically reshaped the old ideal of a unified civil service, and are being extended to ensure competitive tendering for a wide range of civil service professional functions such as economists and engineers. New Zealand went even further under the former Labour government, which drastically slimmed down central government, leaving its agencies with more clearly defined functions and criteria of success. A similar logic has informed the replacement of public ownership with regulated private companies. Utilities such as telecommunications were in theory meant to regulate themselves, with a degree of parliamentary oversight. In practice this often led to a lack of clarity about objectives, a conflict of interest for the planners, and a cosy determination of disputes. The general character of these new approaches is a more rigorous attempt to create precise microincentives for institutions and individuals in them to improve performance.[3]

4   The fourth general shift has been to take funding away from providers and towards consumers, justified in part by the argument that consumer choice can act as a cost discipline on

providers. Examples include rent subsidies, food stamps and vouchers for transport or training which can be used with either public or private providers. In the USA, for example, a remarkable 70 per cent of the federal assistance that reaches non-profit organizations comes in the form of vouchers.

5   The fifth general theme, in some respects informing all the others, is the introduction of competition, whether internal to the public sector or with external agencies, as a way of disciplining costs and changing behaviour to promote a more responsive and entrepreneurial approach.

Each of these reforms has been part of a much larger shift away from the 'administrative tinkering' that characterized public sector reform for several decades, and away from the presumption in favour of administrative rationality. Although cost was the pressure point for change, reforms were only possible because of a deeper sense that the expanded governments of the postwar years had failed, and that failure was at least in part a predictable consequence of ill-conceived structures and misplaced incentives. Failure was also seen as fundamentally bound up with the excessive discretion left to professionals and experts. In the words of Theodor Mars, 'failure was met routinely by the demand for more . . . powers . . . What rationality had come to mean in practice was the parcelling out of decisions to professional groups whose judgement was immune to challenge. It was doctors, teachers and engineers who decided in practice what was to be done. Everyone else was left merely paying the bills.'[4]

The reform agendas were therefore based on a radically different view: in place of administration the market became the paradigm of efficiency. In place of the judgement of professionals, government came to define precise packages of services for delivery by the teachers and doctors, in what Jacques Derrida has called the 'post(al) state'. In place of peer assessment, there would be objective standards of assessment, oriented to outputs rather than inputs. Overall, the models would be those of large throughput service industries rather than of traditional government.

Running through many of these measures has been a new version of the belief that structure determines performance. Predictably, each step has engendered new problems. For example, by giving more weight to management control over finance (and to the power of accountants within organizations), than to more subtle and subjective measures appropriate for needs-based public services, quality has inevitably been vulnerable: new concerns have then followed to ensure that quality is guaranteed through incentives or disciplines. In a similar way, the division between ends and means has often resulted in policy makers devising unworkable strategies, since truly slimmed-down strategic cores are no match for the agencies they are meant to control (one of the reasons why much of business moved away from the model of having a separate corporate strategy department). As a result, there is now a renewed concern for how strategy can be reintegrated into the experience of practice.

The New Consumerism

It is partly because of such problems that the focus of reform has shifted. Despite the failure of both the Reagan and Thatcher administrations to cut more than a little from the bedrock, welfare areas of the public sector, two factors have turned the agenda away from spending cuts towards the quality of what is provided.

One has been the fear that cuts in the 'productive' public services – infrastructure, training, science – may undermine national economic comparative advantage (the same fear has become significant in post-Proposition 13 California). No one has constructed a convincing econometric case to prove the Thatcherite argument that public spending crowds out private investment and hinders economic growth.[5] All that can be said for certain is that those countries which have cut spending most severely – notably the UK – continue to be dogged by slow growth.

But the more important factor shifting the terms of debate has been steadily mounting public concern about standards of service, and the decline of public standards relative to what is available from the private sector. This concern, apparent in Sweden, Germany and the USA as much as in Britain, means that consumerism is now the starting point for almost any discussion of the public sector, whether on the left or the right.

On the left there has been an increasingly lively debate about empowerment through statutory rights, compensations, ombudsmen and commissions to oversee bureaucracies. Greater external transparency has been advocated to ensure that end users are fully aware of their entitlements, that decisions are made in more accountable ways, and that the top-down mass provision of the past is replaced by a more reciprocal development of services between users and providers. It has been argued that the same energies now being devoted to internal management control should be devoted to making services accessible and accountable to users. The etymology of the word 'public' – with links to 'publicity' and 'publishing' – is being implicitly recalled.

On the right the debate is now dominated by the case for contractualism and by the plethora of charters which seek to define the terms of the relationship between providers and users: John Major's sole distinctive addition so far to the Thatcherite legacy. Their claim is that enforceable contracts can mimic some of the effects of the market, and empower the consumer where public services have something of the character of natural monopolies, thus constraining the introduction of competition. The underlying principle is that law and contract are better mechanisms for regulating quality and disciplining providers than regulation or bureaucratic control.

This new approach exemplifies both the strengths and weaknesses of consumerism in the public sector. Its strength is that it gives genuinely enforceable powers to the end user, rather than depending on often very distant democratic channels as a sufficient means of accountability; contracts can also make decision making and priorities more transparent. Its weakness is that, whereas in the market, at least in theory, people enter contracts as equals, in the public sector it is only through political action that people can influence what goes into the contract. That contracts do not in themselves redress the imbalance of power between user and provider has already become apparent in recent reforms, whose main effect has been to make it easier for providers rather than users to opt out: for the doctor to close lists to 'costly' patients, for the school to reject children with learning difficulties or for training bodies to keep clear of special needs training.

The extension of the market model also has other weaknesses. In the market users pay directly for services, whereas in the public sector there may be little overlap between those who vote and pay for services and those who use them. In the market it is always clear who the consumer is, whereas in the public sector it is rarely clear whether the 'true' consumer is the parent or the child, the chronic patient or the occasional patient. These theoretical problems exacerbate the practical problems endemic to the introduction of contracts and markets. Costs often rise as spending on marketing, accounting and consultancy takes off. Competition can drive costs up, as commercial broadcasters repeatedly discovered when they competitively bid film prices far above what public service broadcasters had ever paid. The same experience in health drove the head of BUPA, Britain's main private health care provider, to warn in 1986 that private medicine was 'threatened by commercialism'. In the USA, one result of having to allocate costs to individuals is that administration accounts for 22 per cent of total health expenditure, far more than in other countries.

Perhaps a more fundamental flaw with consumerist and contractualist models, however, is that there are very real informational barriers to the exercise of genuine consumer sovereignty in the choice of doctors or schools. Ironically, it is usually the state that has to take responsibility for providing information to make choices meaningful, and to ensure that those without highly developed social and cultural competences are able to use their rights. In general, markets tend to work well where there is good, cheap and comprehensible consumer information, where the costs of making bad choices are not high, and where tastes are diverse: they work well, in other words; for hi-fi or food, and badly where these conditions do not apply, as for health where information is personal, complex and costly.[6]

The Philosophical Roots of Consumerism

Underlying much of the consumerist agenda is a model of society drawn from neoclassical economics. It is a world of perfect information and sovereign individual consumers, a world in which the only incentives are monetary and the only discipline that of competition. This model has virtues as well as defects. Some of the disciplines of economics have been useful for the public sector, none more, perhaps, than the concept of opportunity cost: the idea that every choice implies that other choices are forgone, an idea that has often been absent from public sector organizations, with their rudimentary mechanisms for comparing capital plans. Similarly, a stricter application of the principle of fiscal neutrality might prove highly egalitarian, since it would remove the privileges which accrue to those benefiting from a university education, the subsidies for road travellers and the enormous tax benefits for homeowners.

In many cases, too, there may well be a case for shifting parts of the public sector if not into the market then at least into mechanisms which give citizens more transparent links between what they pay and what they receive.

But the economics which provides the theoretical model for consumerism has become less convincing the further it has been taken. It has proven subject, you could say, to its own law of diminishing returns, unable to deal effectively with the subtleties of the various goods and services which have accumulated in the public sector. For example, because economics has no models for ethical motivation it cannot explain how the sector has arrived where it is: either why people have worked for lower salaries than they would have earned elsewhere, or why people have consistently voted for its redistributive effects.[7] It has little to say about 'public service ethics',[8] or the ethos of particular professions. Similarly, the 'transactions' view of much public sector economics, which reduces all relationships to exchange, misses the extent to which all societies work in groups and institutions dependent on collective learning and culture. Again, because the model cannot explain the ethos of professions and services and their corporate cultures, it is flawed as a guide to reform.

In general, the predominant models of value are those of the consumer goods market, whereas the economics of social goods is dominated by externalities – the wider benefits of a service that are not captured by the immediate consumer. These have been repeatedly questioned by economists, primarily because they are hard to specify. But it is hard to see how this excuses ignoring them altogether, for such shared values and benefits are fundamental to public provision – whether in the form of the common benefits of containing contagious diseases or curing schizophrenia, the general benefits of higher educational standards, or the benefits to friends and relatives that accrue from the provision of community care.

Democracy and Social Cohesion

These weaknesses show up the limits of the consumerist case, which, in its purest forms, promises a full-scale privatization of responsibility, leaving the state as nothing more than a collection of agencies which might just as well be run in the marketplace. Such a model leaves no space for public goods, for shared values, or for any strategic sense of long-term interests that transcend those of an individual. Indeed, like most orthodox economic theory, it explicitly denies one of the most basic facts of all human history, namely that people live in and through institutions and societies that necessarily operate on much longer timescales than those of individual desire or need.

In what follows I suggest ways to step beyond consumerism rather than away from it, since a basic consumerism is necessary for the legitimacy of any service in an advanced industrial society. My aim is to show how pluralism can be fostered within and around the boundaries of the state, enabling the state to redefine its role away from that of father-figure, providing and operating and bearing full responsibilities, and towards a role at one remove from services: overseeing, cajoling and encouraging, fostering a degree of variety within a fixed framework that is the minimum required for social solidarity.

Its starting point is democracy, the first victim of much recent reform and a word that is almost wholly absent from the consumerist case. Democracy has been a fashionable target for attack as a distorting force, either for promoting the coercion of the few by the many to force up provision,[9] or because of the middle classes' habit of hijacking transfers because of their position as swing voters, or again because of the supposedly inherent tendency of democratic bidding to create inflationary pressures. Many of these claims have turned out to be rather less substantial than they seemed. But for better or worse, and despite the weaknesses of democratic procedures, these remain the primary mechanism for determining the provision of social goods. Unless voters can be persuaded by practical and moral arguments that resources should be spent in the public sector, high-quality provision is simply not possible.

The democratic dimension of the public sector is rarely as simple as it might seem. Contrary to many of the assumptions of those who have attacked democracy in recent decades, electorates regularly vote for lower public spending. Benefits are often concentrated on fairly small, and poor, parts of the electorate even if this is not the case in the USA. Middle-class capture of welfare states may appear at first sight unjust, but it does have some beneficial and ultimately egalitarian effects if it means that the middle classes continue to advocate generous universal provision.[10] More fundamentally, too, recent history has not shown that elected governments have an incurable addiction to inflation: on the contrary, it could equally be said that many have become addicted to deflationary policies.

Democracy's effects can rarely be predicted from one-dimensional models of human nature. It can be an unpredictable tool, particularly when electorates are asked to make decisions about public provision only through the very blunt procedures of party voting. For the purposes of this argument, however, two issues stand out. One is that, if publics are to be given a proper democratic say in the forms and levels of public provision, democratic procedures will have to become as flexible and sophisticated as those of the market which offers itself as an alternative. This may mean a full-scale hypothecation of taxes, leaving electorates greater scope to determine the real spending levels of health, education or housing. It may mean a far greater use of consultation and referenda procedures, as nearly happened in Oregon over health care reform, albeit with some highly problematic results. It may require a far more expert involvement by legislatures in ensuring that there are countervailing forces to the powers of professionals and other industrial vested interests involved in public provision.

These are some of the formal requirements of a more advanced democracy. But for those who seek a regeneration of public provision, it will be equally necessary to revitalize the ethical and communitarian arguments that are as essential to collective provision as the self-interest in what is often a more economically rational way of providing public goods. Unless people feel part of a community, and unless they feel that the public sector is not only a set of delivery agencies but also a means of improving social cohesion – through the everyday experience of sharing surgeries, schools and bus stops that makes society more than an agglomeration of individuals – then it is less likely that they will be prepared to pay for it. Moreover, and this is a crucial point where public ethics are often at odds with those of the professionals, unless they feel that others are also contributing to the common good, meeting obligations as well as taking advantage of rights, their own incentive to care will diminish, and they will be less prepared to pay for the needs of others, and for actions that give weight to substantive as well as formal equality.

This issue is central because more money is likely to be spent on health and education regardless of politics, both because of the effects of cost disease and because of the well-documented propensity of people to spend more of their income on these goods as they become more prosperous. But whether it is spent through the market, with fragmenting effects on everyday social life, or through collective provision will be an important factor in shaping the extent of community and the extent to which interests are felt to be shared.[11] There will undoubtedly be strong pressures on governments to solve their public finance problems by passing provision out to the marketplace, particularly in such costly fields as pensions and health.

Despite its flaws, economics and economic rationality retain their ideological hegemony at least in part because we still lack a fully formed communitarian theory that fits the complexities of the modern world, and which provides a sufficient theoretical foundation for public provision. There has been surprisingly little analysis of how the institutions of everyday life, from the park to the bus, engender social solidarity, and little about how their decay, or changing behaviour by those working within public services, undermines community. We also lack strong enough arguments for people in the wealthy suburbs of New York – or London – to care enough to pay for the needs of others, except through the occasional altruistic impulses of charity.

But if stronger public social philosophies do develop, they will gain support only if, in place of the monolithic and standardized provision of the past, they can offer not only convincing arguments about quality and the containment of costs, but also a distinctive sense of pluralism. They will need, in other words, to distinguish the right's argument that the market is a sufficient means to pluralism from an alternative that sees pluralism as dependent both on the market and on how people are protected from the market. A true pluralism depends, in other words, on the coexistence of many different modes of social organization, each with its own values, rules of distribution and criteria of success.[12] It is diametrically opposed to the assumption of modern economics that all values are commensurate.

Art, health, education, care and research are concerned with different kinds of value than those that can be reduced to money and exchange, so that any imposition of the market introduces damaging distortions. In a genuinely plural society, by contrast, there is recognition of the distinct values of the journalist and the broadcaster, the doctor and the teacher, the midwife and the poet. A pluralism of this kind sees the public sector less as a bureaucratic monolith and more as a protective umbrella within which different kinds of relationship can be sustained: able, too, to contain some of the voluntarist arguments made by the right in the USA (where half the adult population is estimated to give five hours a week to voluntary causes) for community self-help where possible, even if government responsibility remains the indispensable provider of last resort. Ideas of this kind are not new. They recall the ideas of guild socialism and Durkheim's arguments linking social solidarity and the self-regulation of professions, and all the many attempts throughout this century to devise non-bureaucratic alternatives to the market. What perhaps gives them new strength now is that they go with the grain of business organization, where in the 1900s, or 1920s they appeared to go completely against the dominant ideas of efficient organization.

The Public Service Ethic

It was an understandable reaction against paternalistic, technocratic conventional wisdoms that made the professions come under attack from all sides during the 1960s, 1970s and 1980s. From the left they came to be seen as privileged and unaccountable despots. From the right they were attacked as prime examples of provider capture.

Few could dispute that professions have often become highly privileged vested interests. Professions, like bureaucracies, have a tendency to distort provision, to maximize budgets and to minimize accountability. But it is hard to point to any time in history when the effective provision of many social goods has not depended on highly committed, independent bodies of professionals. Often their motivation has been ethical as much as material, and their sense of themselves as professionals has been based both on a complex of responsibilities (such as those of the Hippocratic oath, which balances the doctor's monopoly of information with a set of duties to the patient) and on a strong public service ethos. No one has yet come up with a better model.

Yet it is precisely this ethos which has been badly eroded in recent years. Some professional groups – notably in the civil service and in education – have effectively been proletarianized, treated by their employer, the state, as wage workers like any other. Their relative status has declined rapidly compared to the private sector. As a result, their unions have become increasingly militant, steeped in the language and practices of industrial trade unions. Industrial action has been used against users, and militancy has encouraged professional unions bitterly to resist any moves to appraise them or render them accountable, contributing to a spiralling decay of professional ethos and public support.

Although arguments about pay reveal the professions most clearly as self-interested vested interests, they are right to fight on this ground. In a highly materialist society, pay is more than a material reward because it symbolizes the value put on a profession. It is significant, for example, that the relative alienation of the British teaching and social work professions has coincided with the rapid decline in their pay compared to doctors, police and nurses. A return to proper comparability with the private sector would be a far more important long-term guarantee of quality than any one structural reform. But pay on its own is not enough, for the long-term renewal of the professions (and among the professions we should include nurses, engineers, postal workers and civil servants) also depends on a redefinition of their relation to the community as a whole, and not just to their paymasters and their users.

Organizational Reform

The third field for a post-consumerist reform, necessarily accompanying the revival of communitarian arguments and the remotivation of those working in public services, concerns organization. In the past questions of organization provided a natural ground for the left. Institutions like the Post Office, the BBC (seen by Hugh Dalton, an influential British Labour politician in the 1930s and 1940s as the very model of socialist organization) or the NHS were seen as prefigurative, their methods and values ultimately destined to spread to the whole society. Since the 1940s, however, there has been little movement forward, certainly in terms of workable, transferable organizational forms, as opposed to benign aspirations. Discussions of organization now revolve largely around business models, often with little more than a rhetorical nod to the special characteristics of public organizations.

This is unfortunate since some many of the problems of the public sector arise from its use of old business models. In the 1940s, it was the logistical management practices of the army, and the then standard practices of manufacturing industry – oriented to mass production, low-cost sourcing and complex structures of supervision – which dominated the welfare state. It was precisely because these became frozen into elaborate bureaucracies epitomizing the worst of mid-twentieth-century Fordism that the public sector has found it so hard to adapt. Much of the agenda of reform now seems in danger of repeating that history, with the introduction of ever more intensive centralized supervision under the control of accountants, driven by cost control rather than the use of more creative, quality-oriented models of management. Power seems to be shifting away from those involved in the direct provision of a service, towards those who deal only with abstracted statistics: a recipe in many cases (as in manufacturing) for lower quality and less innovation.

If there is to be a new synthesis of market disciplines and models appropriate to the distinctive goals of public service, ideas from business will have to be used with much greater care, and combined with the thinking about human resources, organizational culture and non-monetary incentives which is taking place across the boundaries between public and private sectors. Many public services can, for example, draw on the care and experience not only of full-time employees but also of volunteers, the retired and relatives, not simply to pass costs out, but also to draw on the best mix of different skills. Many of the individual occupations could use a greater autonomy to develop their own distinctive professional cultures, much as the older professions have done. Meanwhile the organizational theorists can use the space for experiment and innovation to test out the ideas emerging from economics which seek to analyse the values of enduring relationships, trust and co-operation, from Charles Sabel, Amitai Etzioni and business theorists such as Rosabeth Moss Kanter, Shoshanna Zuboff and Charles Handy. This is already happening to a substantial extent at state level in the USA, where a new orthodoxy has emerged based on applying some of the conventional wisdoms of modern business management, such as flatter hierarchies, the fostering of leadership rather than management, the use of competition wherever possible, and the pursuit of quality.[13]

Equally important both to the theory and the practice of the public sector will be a commitment to pluralism in delivering and defining services. In many countries, pluralism in the means of delivery is common, and education, health and social services have always been provided on a large scale by non-profit or religious organisations. In Germany health is paid for out of social insurance for provision by doctors in private practice, while in Sweden many social services have been contracted downwards to independent groups of individuals. In the USA some of the most innovative local authorities have drawn on the energies of voluntary and non-profit groups to clean up parks and streets, to manage recycling initiatives and even to audit some of the work of the local state. A degree of competitive neutrality between state, non-profit and private sectors has much to commend it. It helps to draw in new energies and new ways of working, and it ensures a discipline on costs and quality.

But there is also considerable scope for greater pluralism within the state, so long as there is effective monitoring of the quality of outputs. One apparently successful example has been District 4 in Harlem, where the local authority allowed teachers to create distinct specializations – a performing arts school, a traditionalist school, a marine sciences school, a career preparation school – for children to choose from. By most standard criteria of attainment it has been a great success. Models of this kind suggest a very different pluralism to that of the market, as well as avoiding the socially divisive effects inherent in reforms which allow institutions to opt wholly out of the system of public provision. They show that public institutions can be much more porous to the outside world, with schools encouraging pupils to spend more time in community and business organizations, health authorities helping people at the workplace with gyms or even massages, or libraries working with voluntary organizations.

But even variety is not of itself enough. Ultimately, the survival of public services as legitimate meeters of needs for the whole community will depend on feverish innovation to keep up with changing demands, and new structures that allow for risk, enterprise and specialization within the context of universal provision, structures that match tight overall financial control with real autonomy. Here, too, there is a risk that the simple transplanting of market models will be unsuccessful. Success in meeting changing needs is possible only if those closest to the user – the street cleaner, nurse, meals on wheels – are responsible for more than the simple delivery of a specified service.[14] Genuine innovation depends, in other words, on their having the means to work with users to define and redefine changing needs. This reciprocal relationship, which is very different from the passive choice of the marketplace, brings to mind the older meaning of *glasnost* – the voicing that is the corollary of greater openness. Where market exit is not practical, there is no obvious alternative to such a dialogue, even if at first it may be hard to match viable new practices with the competences of providers.

Typically, governments take something between a third and a half of all wealth created in modern industrial societies. About half of this again is devoted to the public services, to health and education, social security transfers and housing. As such the very scale of the public sector makes it difficult to ignore; certainly no serious political contender can afford not to have a coherent view of how it should be run.

For the parties of the left, which have consistently argued for the public sector to expand, and which have built their voting strength around it (to such an extent that it has often been hard to appreciate the urgency of reform), the need is all the greater. Unfortunately, much of the thinking about change has come from elsewhere, from those not naturally disposed towards collective provision.

This would be a serious problem if the reform process had come to an end. Instead the reimagination or reinvention of government has only just begun. Across the world the rethinking of every element of government, of what it does, how it does it, how its people are motivated and how its users are empowered, implies a continuing revolution which is unlikely to be the exclusive property of any one ideological tradition. This is one reason

why the consumerist move has been a necessary but not a sufficient basis for renewal. It takes market models beyond their
point of relevance and ignores the other elements needed for
effective public provision – a well-motivated workforce, well-
developed moral arguments for provision to others, and a strongly
rooted culture of innovation and pluralism to prevent stagnation
and bureausclerosis. Consumerism is not enough because the
interests of consumers, of providers and of electors are rarely
identical. Efficiency depends on a balance between them. A policy
that is concerned only with the power of people as consumers
erodes both the ethos of the providers and the quality of democratic debate. A policy that is concerned only with the providers
engenders inefficiency and complacency. A policy that overem-
phasizes the democratic process may generate more resources but
only at the cost of lower quality. That is why, as in all organizational matters, what is ultimately at issue is not the best blueprint,
or the single organizing principle, but the best balance.

All forms of public provision are in this sense part of a social
contract: an endlessly renegotiated deal between state, individuals
and communities. To work such deals must balance people's
selfishness and their sociability, their rights and their responsibilities. That is why, in the final analysis, public sectors are not
sustainable either as one-way systems of provision from a benign
state to a passive population, or as simple agencies that meet
demands. Those are models fit for societies which have given up
the ghost, communities that have lost any reason to cohere, and
in which the very idea of the public becomes little more than a
label, ever more detached from its own origins.

Notes

1 G. Schieber and J. P. Poullier, 'International health care expenditure
   trends: 1987', *Health Affairs*, 8, 1989, pp. 169–77.
2 *OECD Observer*, April 1991.
3 One of the fullest expositions is in David Osborne and Ted Gaebler,
   Reinventing Government, Addison-Wesley, New York, 1992.
4 T. F. Mars, 'Public sector organisation: where next?', *IDS Bulletin*,
   vol. 23, no. 4., 1992.

5   This is shown conclusively by Francis Castles and Steve Dowrick in 'The impact of government spending levels on medium term economic growth in the OECD, 1960–85', *Journal of Theoretical Politics*, 1990.

6   Nicholas Barr, 'Economic theory and the welfare state: a survey and interpretation', *Journal of Economic Literature*, XXX, June 1992, p. 750.

7   See Amitai Etzioni, *The Moral Dimension*, Free Press, New York, 1988.

8   See Christopher Pollitt, *Managerialism and the Public Services*, Blackwell, Oxford, 1990, chapter 6.

9   Famously in Anthony Downs, *An Economic Theory of Democracy*, Harper and Row, New York, 1957.

10 See Julian LeGrand, 'The middle-class use of the British social services', in R. Goodin and J. LeGrand (eds), *Not Only the Poor: the middle classes and the welfare state*, Allen and Unwin, London, 1987.

11 The argument of Robert Nozick in opposing public provision even if it leads to better outcomes provides the purest opposition to this, an attack on collective modes of decision making. *Anarchy, State and Utopia*, Blackwell, Oxford, 1974.

12 See Michael Walzer, *Spheres of Justice*, Harvard University Press, Cambridge, Mass., 1983.

13 Osborne and Gaebler, op. cit.

14 A recent survey is given by Hywel Griffiths, 'Community resource development: a strategy for the 1990s', *Policy Studies*, autumn 1990.

8

RETICULATED ORGANIZATIONS: THE BIRTH AND DEATH OF THE MIXED ECONOMY

During the 1980s government enterprises worth an estimated $185 billion were sold to the private sector worldwide in much the fastest redrawing of the boundaries of state and market that the world has ever seen. This essay offers an explanation of why this happened and why such diverse industries had previously been brought into public ownership, focusing in particular on the 'network' or 'reticulated industries' that have always made up the heart of the mixed economy

By the 1980s, the typical industrialized country had roughly 10 per cent of GDP in state enterprises, and between 6 and 8 per cent of all employment (the one significant exception was the USA with only 2 per cent of employment). The UK was typical in that public enterprises accounted for 10 per cent of GDP and 16 per cent of gross fixed capital formation. It was also typical in that the boundaries of this sector had continually fluctuated: in 1919, for example, nationalization even extended to the pubs of Carlisle to stop them overselling beer.

Between the mid-nineteenth century and the middle of the twentieth huge swathes of industry were taken into public control across the world under models varying from those of Taiwan (where Sun Yat-sen's ideas on the role of public ownership were highly influential),[1] through those of Nehru and Nkrumah to

those of the postwar reconstruction in countries like France and
Britain. State involvement ranged along a continuum from direct
integration in civil services (like the Post Office until 1969),
through arm's-length ownership to strategic oversight. Different
parts of the state could be dominant: in Britain (with the exception
of London) gas, electricity and water were run by municipal
authorities until nationalized after World War II. The Manchester
Ship Canal of 1891 was set up jointly by municipal corporations
and private stockholders, while bodies like the Metropolitan
Water Board were run by boards representing both local authorities and users. In France there was the peculiar evolution of the
economie mixte with considerable power held at regional and
local level even after the waves of nationalization in the 1940s.
In the USA most of the utilities were organized, and came to be
regulated, at state level. In countries like Italy considerable power
was exercised through state holding companies. Despite these
differences, however, what is remarkable by historical standards
is how similar the various mixed economies were from Chile to
Finland, covering a similar set of network and strategic industries,
and how dissimilar they were from earlier models such as the
state-owned papyrus makers of Ancient Egypt or Colbert's manu-
factories in seventeenth-century France.

Even as it spread under governments of all political colours,
however, the mixed economy always remained the subject of
fierce political debate. For fifty years until the 1980s the focus
of the debate was the precise location of the boundary between
public and private, but it never reached any firm conclusions
because, as we shall see, there were no firm theoretical grounds
for defining the boundary. Instead, as a broad generalization,
attitudes followed from ideological positions. Labour movements
tended to see the publicly owned part of the economy as prefigurative[2] – a demonstrator of the virtues of public ownership and
planning which should be progressively extended (with intervention in private industry, by contrast, often viewed as an illegitimate subsidy for capital).[3] Nationalist parties tended to view
public ownership as the concomitant of nation building, a focus
for national economic energy, a counterweight to multinationals
and a necessary lever for an effective state, and were therefore

content to rest with the commanding heights of the economy. Conservative and liberal parties tended to see public ownership more as a necessary evil where natural monopolies existed, where the essential nature of goods (such as water) precluded the instabilities of market provision, or where private industry failed to respond to fiscal and monetary incentives: at the limit they believed that the state should only run what the markets refused to run.[4] Harold Macmillan, for example, felt quite at ease in writing in the 1930s that the 'socialist remedy . . . should be accepted . . . where it is obvious that private enterprise has exhausted its social usefulness'.[5]

One of the striking features of these positions is the extent to which they were political rather than economic in inspiration. The economic theories of public goods and imperfect competition, and the huge Soviet planning literature, only took form in the 1920s and 1930s well after many industries had come into public ownership. The Marxist tradition was famously silent on how public enterprises should be run, and the first formal definition of what a public corporation should be in Britain came from the Crawford Committee on the BBC, hardly an obvious model for industrial organization even if Hugh Dalton was later to claim it as such, and typical in that its charter set out the corporation's purpose around extremely vague notions of national interest. In the absence of a clear theory, the public enterprises tended to accumulate their logic from practice. Raymond Williams' comment about broadcasting, that 'the institutions and social policies which get established in a formative, innovative stage – often ad hoc and piecemeal in a confused and seemingly marginal area – have extraordinary persistence into late periods if only because they accumulate techniques, experience, capital and what come to seem prescriptive rights', could be applied right across the public sector.

The Reticulated State

Although public ownership covered a wide range of industries, some taken over for strategic reasons and some to assist with decline, I want to focus on what has always been the core of the public sector: the 'reticulated' or network industries. These are industries which branch down into everyday life, often with direct physical links to every home or business (as with gas, electricity, telephones or water), or direct delivery (as with the postal service). They are particularly significant for four reasons: they were the first nationalized industries, the first regulated industries, the pioneers of many of the forms of modern business organization, and the first industries to generate a debate about privatization and deregulation.

Their original significance derived from their role in shaping the boundaries of states' military power. But in the modern period the involvement of states deepened for economic reasons. In Germany half of all investment in railways up to 1850 came from government, well before Bismarck's nationalization. In France, where the majority of investment in canals and railways was public, it was 'thanks to the support given by the state that this sector was spared from the bankruptcies and almost spared from the technical failures which it frequently experienced abroad'.[6] Even in the USA the telegraph industry was launched with a £30,000 grant from Congress.[7]

State support often turned into ownership. In France and Germany railways and telegraph were easily integrated into the state after a period of private ownership (according to Werner Sombart, in Germany the postal services and railways were 'only the civil sections of the army', with generals often acting as senior managers). In Britain the Post Office was run by government, prior to the nationalization first of the telegraph, then of the telephones and, half a century later, of the railways. In Japan the majority of railways, and telecommunications were state owned until the 1980s.

Where ownership remained in private hands, governments had to devise novel methods of regulation. These methods, including many still used in the USA and elsewhere, can be traced to Britain's Regulation of Railways Act 1844, which established powers to cap private companies' rates and to impose social obligations. These were justified at the time by William Gladstone in a sophisticated argument which explained why the character of the railway market would preclude competition. Nominally, regulations were concerned with only a few parameters, such as price and profit. Over time, however, under the influence of regulations which set standards and rules, the various private network operators came to take on much of the character of civil service. AT&T in the USA was probably the classic case, and as near to a civil service with traded shares as the world has ever seen.

It was these companies which pioneered many of the forms of industrial organization later adopted in private industry.[8] They had to innovate because when they were first created in the 1830s and 1840s, in the parallel spread of railways and telegraph, and later in the spread of electricity, gas and water distribution, they had no precedents in the private sector. Their sheer scale, both in terms of capital and labour employed and in terms of their geographical spread, was of a new order. By the end of the nineteenth century, they were among the largest institutions of their time, with a scale and reach exceeding that of many national governments. They were in all cases pioneers of the 'visible hands' of active planning, forecasting and co-ordination which came to replace the invisible hand of the market. In France, for example, by the 1880s gas and electricity were the second- and third-largest companies. In the USA Western Union and later AT&T were the largest companies of their times, massive by comparison with the firms of even a few decades before. In Britain, too, according to Chandler, the 'British railroad companies were by far the largest business enterprises . . . during the 19th century'.[9]

In retrospect it is clear that these firms were in many respects more like police forces (which date from the same period) and civil services than other private companies which only later took on this reticulated character with national banking branch networks, cinema chains and franchised fast-food stores. Indeed, such national private sector companies were simply not conceivable until national reticulated infrastructures had been built, whether by private or public companies, to distribute goods and to communicate.

As the leading organizations of their time, in terms of their scale and scope, their degree of rationalization, and their immersion in the scientific principles of the time, it seemed self-evident in most of the world that the network industries should come under the umbrella of modernizing government, whether national or local. Governments' techniques of organization, often developed in colonial administration and the military, were at least on a par with the most advanced forms of private organization, particularly as mass wars like World War I sharply increased governments' organizational capacities. The military had long before pioneered most of the forms of modern industry: the detailed separation and specification of functions, and standardization and logistical organization of large quantities over space and time. Mass production, interchangeable parts and complex divisions of labour were familiar in military industries long before they took root more widely. At a local level, too, municipal authorities enjoyed advantages of organization over their private counterparts. In water, for example, by the second half of the century, municipal authorities enjoyed far better access than private firms to information and capital.[10]

In short, when the new networks were formed it was natural that they should be close to government and informed by governmental rationalities. It was also the case that the special economic and technological characters of the network industries made them particularly obvious candidates for rationalization and development by states. The fragmented nature of some of the industries, in stark contrast to others, was an obvious barrier to modernization: in Britain, for example, electricity was constrained by incompatibilities, gas by the failure of the many local companies to collaborate on research and development. When industries were returned to the private sector, as the railways and coal were after World War I, the effect was usually to delay necessary restructuring and investment.

In the absence of effective agencies for restructuring in the private sector, government's role was almost self-evident. In Britain, for example, the Labour nationalization programme of 1945–51 was largely based on reports from committees of inquiry set up by previous governments, Reid on coal, Heyworth on gas and MacGowan on electricity. The same pattern of apparently non-partisan policy can be found throughout the century. Nationalization of the Forestry Commission took place under Lloyd George in 1919, while other nationalizations – of the BBC in 1926, the Central Electricity Board in 1927, the London Passenger Transport Board in 1933, the air services under BOAC in 1939, Rolls Royce and what came to be British Leyland in the 1970s – all took place under the Conservatives.

But there was also a more fundamental reason why the state seemed a natural owner. The network industries were designed to provide on a mass scale highly standardized products and services. Their tasks were very similar to the roles being taken on by governments as they began to offer services in employment, health and education. Their employment of huge workforces to provide services paralleled precisely the burgeoning bureaucracies of education and welfare. Often the languages began to overlap, as investments in rural railways or telephone lines, and the cross-subsidies between high- and low-usage parts of the networks, were justified socially. The result was that organizational logics which had been developed by states were readily transferred into the reticulated public organizations, exemplified most clearly perhaps in the way that the nascent telephone industry was explicitly organized around principles derived from the Royal Signals Corps.

Public ownership of these first great network industries established much of the later rationale for public ownership. For Bernard Shaw, for example, 'the extraordinary success of the Post Office, which according to the Manchester School should have been a mess of incompetence and jobbery, had ... shown the perfect efficiency of state enterprise ... and the enormous convenience and cheapness of socialistic charges'.[11] The rationale was, in other words, largely economic, or rather techno-economic, in that the economic characteristics flowed from the nature of network technologies. All of the networks shared economic tendencies: high fixed and relatively low marginal costs; long investment lead times; and dependence on various types of right of way. These tended to render competition deeply unstable, since owners of competing electricity, telegraph or railway networks would drive prices down to marginal costs until one or other succumbed and a monopoly or cartel could be formed (as was the case in the US railways in the 1870s and the German railways in 1846). As a result, investment was irregular and uncertain, bankruptcies common and services unreliable. To the then burgeoning engineering community, which did so much to influence the prevailing climate of opinion, it was evident that a more rational model of organization was needed, to be achieved either through municipal or national ownership, or alternatively through the kind of regulated monopoly that AT&T engineered in the early years of this century.

The Argument of Monopoly

In a regularly quoted sentence from the *Wealth of Nations*, Adam Smith describes the benefits of public subsidy for canals and roads, the networks of his time. What is less often noticed is that there has never been a fully fledged economic theory for these sectors: in most of Smith's successors one can find only a few sentences on those sectors which do not fit the standard model. Instead the available theories have always been add-ons, cobbled together from theories of externality and public good, interdependent demand and clubs. Even these have appeared only in this century, well after the organizing principles, and indeed many of the regulatory priniciples, were in place. Even now the emerging network economics rests ill at ease in a discipline based on methodological individualism. This contrasts sharply with the theories of planning which, for all their subsequent failings, accumulated a breadth and depth, and an obvious practical base in the experience first of war and second of the planned economies.

Despite these theoretical gaps, however, there has, at least since the 1930s, been a reasonably coherent case for public ownership of network industries, drawing loosely on the work of Alfred Marshall, and more directly on A. C. Pigou's analysis of private and public goods and the emerging theories of imperfect competition and monopoly. Three sets of arguments stand out, and continue to be invoked to this day:

1 Networks are natural monopolies; the optimal size of firms is large, and there are substantial economies of scale (often more precisely economies of density or penetration). Competition can promote an inefficient multiplication of standards (in Australia, for example, railway gauges were not standardized until the 1950s).

2 Networks are producers of quasi-public goods. In other words, they have important spin-off effects not directly captured by their immediate consumers: dynamic effects on economic growth and on social well-being. Some of the goods are also 'club' goods, where benefits grow according to the number of consumers (both directly as with telephones or fax machines, and because of the indirect benefits of standardization and scale).

3 Networks supply essential goods on which the whole of economic and social life is dependent. Any disruption to supply would threaten the whole economy; public ownership was thus justified as a precondition for economic security (a justification which could be extended to non-network industries such as steel or coal).

Each of these arguments makes the claim that network industries are concerned with distinct types of value, more social and public, and more defined by interconnection, than those of other industries. In precisely the same way, arguments for public ownership of other types of industry have also been based on ideas about value. For strategic industries, for example, proponents of public ownership have pointed to the cumulative nature of the values they produced, their increasing returns to scale and their dynamic comparative advantages, which render the market's valuation of an industry and its returns inadequate. More recently, proponents of defensive types of ownership, in steel and ships in the 1960s and 1970s, have typically used arguments posed in terms of a social value, such as the cost of sustaining high unemployment in a region, which overrides the narrow economic values of commercial decisions.

What is significant about these arguments is that they assume that there is little need to worry about institutional forms. Since private monopoly tends towards exploitation of the consumer, it is assumed that public monopoly must be a better alternative. To take just one, early example, W. Clarke in the Fabian essays of 1889 is typical in that he deduces from an analysis of the new trend of concentration and monopoly both in the network industries and in steel and shipping, the self-evident need for state ownership. The question of the state's competence, or lack of it, rarely arose, and although commentators like Tawney recognized that 'when the question of ownership has been settled the question of administration remains for solution',[12] this was generally seen as a technical issue and hardly likely to be beset by fundamental contradictions.

The Fallacy of Ownership

The case for public ownership was based on an assumption that the legal status of ownership is the central determinant of how property is used and organized. Only an owner can direct, set targets and gather information, safe in the knowledge that there will be no conflict of interest with other stakeholders. Change can be instigated directly, rather than through the thick veil that impedes the use of incentives and directions.

Yet the history of public ownership has been a history of problematic control, of formal power combined with practical impotence: narrowly over such issues as how to set operational guidelines – for example, over pricing or required rates of return for investments; more broadly, because any enterprise locked into a political system is therefore tied to a shifting and not always compatible collection of goals, which may range from price control and employment creation to regional investment.

Such tensions between control and ownership are not unknown in the private sector. Ironically, even at the high point of state ownership the literature on management control and the weakness of ownership, from Berle and Means and many others, was already large. For states, however, the problems are even more severe. Six sets of problems have characterized public ownership of enterprises.

First, there is an endemic problem of discipline. The discipline of bankruptcy is lost and capital cannot be written off. The disciplines on labour are weak because of labour's political power. Even the most elementary right of ownership, alienability, is severely constrained.

Second, the absence of mediation and the dispersal of responsibility that occurs in a 'normal' economy has always caused political problems. Unlike private owners, governments have no alibis for performance: they cannot blane an impersonal market when jobs are cut and services are closed down.

Third, there is a problem of industrial structure. Many third world countries discovered that nationalization gave no control over the key points of economic power, the places where commodity prices were determined. Much the same pressures have constrained state-owned British car firms and French computer manufacturers, which found that they could not operate under the conditions of sovereignty that other arms of the state assume.

Fourth, economic globalization has caused problems. Increasingly, state-owned firms found themselves forced to compete in globalized markets that both reduced the salience of the strategic use of a dominant firm, and weakened the ability of national firms to compete overseas because of the constraints of political control. State ownership seriously compromised the independence of companies like British Telecom or Cable and Wireless in bidding for contracts and competing for markets.

Fifth, there has been a consistent problem of motivation. Little systematic attention was ever given to how managers and employees in public enterprises should be motivated. A vague assumption that the public good would engender a more responsible and committed workforce came to mean little. This was less the case where the culture of work was shaped by some overriding ethos – such as the engineering ethos which was so powerful in many of the network industries, or where face-to-face contact with users gave some meaning to public purpose. Otherwise the public interest turned out to be too diffuse an ideal to motivate.

Sixth, and perhaps most fundamental of all, governments have lacked sufficient organizational and informational capacity fully to govern a large number of enterprises effectively. There is a long history of the successive attempts made in all countries to impose standard accounting and planning procedures in order to mimic some of the workings of a private capital market. The still unresolved debate about appropriate pricing mechanisms can be dated back to the Ecole des Ponts et Chaussées in France in the early nineteenth century. Ever since the early 1960s, British governments have sought a 'rationalisation of control and performance by economic criteria'.[13] Successive White Papers in 1961 and 1967 sought to tighten decision-making criteria, with 'return on capital' and 'marginal cost pricing' rules, where at the time of nationalization there had been little more than the requirement that revenues should be sufficient to cover costs. But all the reforms did little to alter the fundamental structural problems of ownership. In France the 1967 Nova report made a similar attempt to modernize financial reporting and management. Arrays of monitoring systems were introduced, some dependent on external sources, others on internally generated targets, but all beset by a massive and irresolvable informational asymmetry between the controller and the object of control.

The Problem of Control

Most of these problems can be subsumed under the more general problem of control: governments in the twentieth century have been engaged in a series of complex experiments into the extent and possibility of control in both society and economy, as they have sought to find out whether the monopoly of power and sovereignty which parliaments and ministries appear to have can be translated into useful control. Enterprises operating in markets represent just one field in which the limitations of control have become apparent, as attention has turned away from the arguments for state ownership and towards the practical competences of governments and the problems of information gathering, of where to locate strategic thinking and intelligence, of how to avoid overload, and of how to deal with the more general problems of control common to large bureaucratic organizations whether in the private or the public sector.

One effect has been a surprising convergence of developments in both private and public sectors. For state bureaucracies the same logic which at one time fostered empire building has instead led to support for privatization as a means of retaining power while devolving responsibility. For civil services it may become more attractive to retain overall strategic oversight, and some regulatory powers, while operational responsibility is passed down. For private companies, for similar reasons, direct ownership over all aspects of production has been gradually displaced by the techniques of franchising, subcontracting and licensing, all of which accentuate the market power of the dominant company by allowing it to free itself from the constraints of ownership.

Theoretical Erosion

While practical problems chipped away at the confidence of state enterprises, their theoretical supports were also proving vulnerable. Significantly, it was in the network industries that the erosion of the case was most pronounced and that the most intellectual work was done on alternatives to state ownership and monopoly. The process began in telecommunications as a series of regulatory judgements and economic articles in the USA gradually undermined the claim that telecommunications was a natural monopoly. The networks' monopolies were challenged from the outside inwards as power generation, water purification, gas production, telecommunications equipment, value added services and premium postal services, all came to be seen as potentially competitive within a relatively normal marketplace.

As this happened, a crucial change took place in the ways in which the values produced by networks were conceived. Where originally these had been understood as producers of standardized services, ones indeed whose very virtue was their simplicity in standardizing voltages, bandwidths and plugs, by the 1960s this was ceasing to be an accurate description. Telecommunications could provide a range of differentiated and customized services, value added services, mobile services and subscription services. In energy, post and railways, too, more specialized needs and models of production were appearing, ranging from small-scale renewable energy to commuter trains built to function like offices.

Whereas in an earlier period the necessary concentration, rationalization and standardization of network industries had been in tune with what governments had become used to in their own work, by the 1970s this was no longer true. The necessary restructuring appeared to go against the grain of normal governance, towards flexibility and devolution, variety and entrepeneurialism, and towards much closer links with users in the definition of services. At the same time competition in international markets required sharp cutbacks in labour and joint ventures with overseas companies.

The historic shift towards more flexible, user-oriented forms of organization of network industries seemed impossible to achieve within the institutions and cultures that had been bequeathed. The civil service cultures of provision according to bureaucratically determined and stable levels of service had to be replaced by a more customer-oriented approach. In a sense the solution was obvious: since the competences of states were no longer suitable for the problem at hand, the problems were passed out to institutions which had the competence to run advanced reticulated forms of organization.

Since the earlier takeover of these core reticulated industries, the private sector had, as it were, leapfrogged the public. Its models of reticulated organization had become far more sophisticated, involving devolution of responsibility to operating units, flexibility in production, the involvement of users in the definition of services, and novel combinations of strict financial oversight and operational decentralization. Considerable expertise had been built up with techniques of franchising (a model which can be said to have been invented by the Post Office through its thousands of sub post offices), and the provision of guaranteed levels of service and maintenance. The larger transnational private companies also had the advantage of acting as channels for organizational learning from the world's more dynamic economies. The time was therefore ripe for the superior organizational techniques of the private sector to flow back into the public sector, assisted by neo-liberal ideas which helped to bring what Foucault called 'governmental rationality', the conventional thinking about what administrations can achieve, back into line with governments' true organizational competences.

These various organizational and theoretical factors behind privatization can, of course, be exaggerated. Fiscal necessity was usually a more immediate cause, overriding fears about what markets might do to familiar old institutions. In Britain it was the need to raise money for the Exchequer, and to allow companies to raise capital off the PSBR, which was critical in encouraging privatization of the great network industries. But this was just one factor which converged with many others into a sea change in attitudes and practices that cut across the political spectrum. In the USA the deregulationists who did so much to challenge traditional arguments about networks' natural monopolies began on the left, arguing the consumer case for greater competition against the monolithic bureaucracies of AT&T and the other utilities. In many countries, privatization was supported by trade unions, as in Japan where NTT employees welcomed the prospect of private sector pay. Elsewhere, too, privatization rarely fits into a simple political model of left and right: in India, for example, it has been a means of displacing the Congress Party; in Eastern Europe a mechanism in some cases for old elites to re-establish their power, in others to displace them; in South Africa, along with competitive tendering, a potential means of displacing the white elite.

New Models: Beyond the Mixed Economy

The analysis so far suggests that between the 1960s and 1980s the link between the prevailing approaches to organization, and the types of value which they were designed to control, began to break down. What had been governed industries could no longer be easily governed. Their means and ends were no longer self-evident. The result was the theoretical articulation and practical implementation of two different models for resolving the crisis.

The privatized economy

The first option has been to eliminate the distinction between the types of value associated with network industries and those of normal markets, and to remove the state from any but the most minimal involvement. The goal is a wholly privately owned economy, based predominantly on competitive industries and, where this is not possible (with a very strong presumption that competition can be created in most erstwhile 'natural monopolies'), simple regulation that mimics competitive markets. The light touch regulation of formulae, which set limits for utility prices, is an example. The discipline provided by shareholders on the one hand, and consumers in a competitive market on the other, are taken to be sufficient policers of efficiency. The idea that the state can in any way substitute in determining public interest ends for consumers is rejected.

The regulated economy

The second option can be called the 'regulated economy'. The idea that network industries involve distinct types of value is retained, but matched with a new machinery for control which separates ownership from control, regulation from operation. The ownership structure of the privatized economy is combined with a highly active regulatory state, acting through agencies at arm's length from government itself with wide powers to influence decision making. Utilities are controlled through price limits but also through linking in other goals such as household penetration in the case of telecommunications, quality of service (for example, in water), social provision and regional spread. Regulators can also be given broader strategic power to ensure the development of new technologies or industrial capacity. In short a series of public interests are defined by the state and policed by agencies in what is no longer a mixed economy, but rather a combination of private ownership and public control in which regulations, preferably transparent, define the public interest.

Regulated competition

Neither of these models is yet in place in a pure form, although there is a clear momentum towards them as two poles of a continuum of 'regulated competition'. Both, however, have fundamental flaws. The privatized economy model remains acutely vulnerable to the criticism that it will underprovide public goods and goods with externality effects; even if these can be reflected in taxes or subsidies, government's greater distance from the practical knowledge of these industries will tend to make any such interventions less effective. With environmental issues rapidly entering the world of the utilities through the energy issues of generation and conversation, through the problems of water quality and through the impacts of transport and communications networks on energy usage, this model seems unlikely to prove sustainable. In other respects, too, the attempted depoliticization of the networks inplied by full privatization is already running into obstacles, since although many of the types of value being produced by networks are becoming more differentiated, basic services retain overwhelming preponderance, and are treated by users as different in nature from other services. Another barrier to depoliticization is that, far from passing decision making out of government, one effect of privatization has been to create a new and powerful lobby on government: what could be called a 'privatization complex', a market distortion of government, based on private contractors and other providers dependent on public money.[14]

The fundamental flaws of the regulatory model, by contrast, are primarily informational. Just as finance ministries could rarely know much about the strategic choices or underlying costs of complex networks, so has it proved immensely hard for regulators to get deeply into the information of regulated companies. Such asymmetries may be unavoidable, particularly when in a competitive market companies have stronger arguments for non-disclosure. But even if full information were available, it remains hard to see how regulatory agencies could arrive at adequate and transparent definitions of the public interest when, despite more than a century as a fully fledged discipline, economics can offer no useable concepts of public good or externality.

The problems inherent to these two 'ideal-type' options therefore seem likely to push policy makers in new directions. One set of options would bring a return to greater state involvement, but in new forms.

1　The first would involve a move towards what could be called the 'directive state'. Instead of operating either through ownership or through arm's length agencies, government would define and police overall strategies for the network industries. The traditional strategic role of government would be revived, but in the modern form of the executive agency, able to evolve its own culture and techniques, and empowered to control access to markets in order to impose a relatively small number of social, environmental and technological requirements.

2　The second possible direction of development would be towards a mercantilism of reticulated industries. Their domestic conditions of operation would be determined primarily by their need to compete effectively in other countries. High prices for customers would be justified by the need to generate surplus capital for acquisitions abroad. Private or minority state ownership would be combined with aggressive support by government. Elements of these approaches are already visible in the US government's treatment of AT&T and the regional Bell Operating Companies, in the UK government's treatment of British Telecom and Cable and Wireless, and in arguments surrounding the future organization of gas and electricity industries in a more openly competitive European marketplace, where innovations such as superconductivity will make it technically easier for energy suppliers to distribute energy across very large areas.

3　A third option would be to democratize the concept of the public good. Traditionally, public goods and quasi-public goods have been largely beyond quantification. Externalities, though integrated into cost–benefit analysis techniques, are always in practice experts' estimates. In recent years, however, debates around environmental values have led to the beginnings of a revolution in the concept as public preferences are sought and turned into quantities. The informational tasks of the market in transmitting private preferences are replicated through collective decision making, partly as a way of ensuring legitimacy for decisions, partly as a way of shifting responsibility out from the core of the state. This may be one long-term effect of innovations such as the citizen's charters, which could be turned into tools for making choices about public priorities.

A second set of options, by contrast, would involve a further diminution of direct state involvement.

1   One would be a move towards greater self-regulation. Networks would be governed by legally defined obligations and interests, but rather than being subject to enforcement by a single regulatory agency, the policing function would be passed out to a dispersed auditing profession, required to govern itself according to agreed criteria. To a large extent this is already the case with financial reporting; it is currently spreading rapidly to environmental issues, and may evolve further into areas such as ergonomics, training policy and even decision-making practices. The aim would be to overcome some of the informational asymmetries of the agency model by embedding regulation and public interests more deeply within organizations. The weakness is, of course, that such auditing depends on the genuine independence and public motivation of those doing it.

2   An alternative solution to the informational overload problem that is endemic to government involvement in the economy would redefine government's role away from the totality of what industries do and towards what could be termed their interfaces, such as the service delivered to the home, the interconnection of networks, the terms of competition and the terms of trade or interconnection at an international level. Only at these points would public interests be defined and given regulatory or legal backing, leaving to organizations themselves the problem of ensuring that requirements are met. In embryo this has been the rationale of the Open Network Architecture and Open Network Provision rules for telecommunications in the USA and Europe respectively.

Conclusions

The mixed economy has often been interpreted as a common sense compromise between the extremes of *laissez-faire* and planning. What I have shown is that, in an important set of sectors, it arose rather because the new models of organization that were developing within governments spread into the economy, starting with the great reticulated organizations. These rational, standardizing, technology-driven bodies, organized in national hierarchies with local nodes, became obvious candidates for public ownership because competitive markets without adequate capital were often simply not capable of providing stable levels of service.

Sixty years ago, the two sectors were more obviously in balance, and the Bridgman Committee justified keeping the Post Office within the civil service with the argument that 'overcentralisation, absence of initiative, lack of imagination and failure to give appropriate representation to technical functions are faults which are to be found in the sphere of private as well as government administration'. Since then, however, the balance has tilted decisively away from government. The penetration of the economy by government has gone into reverse and the private sector's competences in reticulated organization have evolved rapidly, providing a practical basis for market ideas to spread beyond more obviously economic functions into government itself, and into everything from prisons to schools and hospitals. In all these parts of the state, internal markets are coming into use, and ideas such as those popularized by David Osborne and Ted Gaebler[15] for introducing competition, performance measurements and incentives into bureaucracies to make them innovative, responsive and entrepreneurial are gaining ground. The momentum is such that it is hard to conceive of any early return to widespread public ownership unless the micro-reform of public servies somehow enables them to jump ahead of conservative private institutions (like the crudely reticulated high street banks, which leave almost no autonomy to branch managers).

This flood of private sector ideas into government can be interpreted, following Harold Perkin, as a victory of the private sector prefessionals over the public sector ones. But it may be better understood as a new twist in the long history of what Jacques Donzelot has called the 'hybridisation of the private and the public, the state and the civil'. The big change in recent years is that, whereas previously the state handed down answers to society's needs, now across many spheres the problems of the state are being devolved so that society becomes implicated in the task of resolving them.[16] This can be seen most dramatically perhaps in the mass privatizations of the Treuhandanstalt in Germany, of Kraus in Czechoslovakia and the Yeltsin government in Russia, more modestly in the hiving off of public enterprises in the West.

If this analysis is correct then the swing away from public ownership is not simply an effect either of medium-term political cycles of the kind that Karl Polanyi and Albert Hirschman have analysed, or of that drunkard's walk of progress, which leads nations from the failures of market-driven systems, to public ownership and back again, with some never-quite-attained happy medium in between that is always overshot. Nor can it be analysed with the distinctions drawn by Michel Albert and others to categorize the different types of modern capitalist society. These cannot explain why, for example, both the German and Japanese governments have felt the need to privatize their telecommunications operators, and why governments of both left and right have restructured their reticulated industries in similar ways. Instead, the changing balance between public and private, state and market solutions, cannot be separated from the organizational forms and competences which each brings to bear. It is with these, and with public and private organizations' practical ability to recognize and solve problems in everything from energy to prisons and from universities to childcare, that any useful argument now has to begin.

Notes

1   See, for example, Robert Wade's account in *Governing the Market: economic theory and the role of government in East Asian industrialisation*, Princeton University Press, Princeton, 1990.

2   Although there were other traditions: see, for example, G. D. H. Cole, *Economic Tracts for the Times*, 1932, chapter 12.
3   Jim Tomlinson, *The Unequal Struggle: British socialism and the capitalist enterprise*, Methuen, London, 1982.
4   A strong line of liberal argument denied the importance of the difference between public and private ownership: Liberal Party, *Britain's Industrial Future*, 1928; J. M. Keynes, 'The means to prosperity', in *Essays in Persuasion*, 1933.
5   Harold Macmillan, *The Middle Way*, Macmillan, London, 1938, p. 239.
6   Quoted in *Cambridge Economic History*, VII, p. 249.
7   Richard B. Du Boff, 'The rise of communications regulation: the telegraph industry 1844–80', *Journal of Communications*, Summer 1984.
8   Alfred Chandler, *The Visible Hand*, Harvard/Bellknap, Cambridge, Mass., 1977.
9   Alfred Chandler, *Scale and Scope*, Bellknap, London, 1990, p. 253.
10 J. Hassan, 'The growth and impact of the British water industry', *Economic History Review*, 38, 1985, p. 546.
11 G. B. Shaw, 'Transition', in *Fabian Essays in Socialism*, 1889, p. 185.
12 R. H. Tawney, *The Acquisitive Society*, London, 1921, p. 149.
13 L. Tivey (ed.), *The Nationalised Industries since 1960*, Allen and Unwin, London, 1973.
14 Paul Starr, *The Limits of Privatization*, Economic Policy Institute, Washington, 1987.
15 David Osborne and Ted Gaebler, *Reinventing Government*, 1991.
16 Jacques Donzelot, 'The mobilisation of society', in G. Burchell *et al.* (eds), *The Foucault Effect*, Harvester, Hemel Hempstead, 1991, p. 178.

9

THE RENEWABLE
ENERGIES OF POLITICS

It is unbelievable how many systems of morals and politics have been successively found, forgotten, rediscovered, forgotten again, to reappear a little later, always charming and surprising the world as if they were new, and bearing witness not to the fecundity of the human spirit but to the ignorance of men.

Alexis de Tocqueville

To succeed in politics you have to have energy: enough not only to defeat your enemies, but also to save yourself from stagnation. These political energies, which movements and parties struggle to command, fall into two categories. Into the first fall those powerful (if exhaustible) energies that come from the dynamic currents of a society: perhaps the confidence of a rising class or a demographic bulge. These are the political equivalents of fossil fuels, forced to the surface by seismic shifts in social structures, and available to anyone with the wit to use them. Into the second category fall more renewable kinds of energy: the enduring values and insights of traditions that transcend the conditions from which they arise, the ideas that inspire and instruct across time, and which can be tapped into to renew the vigour and purpose of movements that have grown too accustomed to power and compromise.

For the world's left, originally defined in the Assembly of 1789 as the force of progress against reaction – that is to say, the force of future energy – the question has always been particularly pertinent: how to harness the strongest new energies to its cause, while also tapping the renewable strengths of the tradition. Now at the close of the century, with the left's parties in decline and disarray, its social bases apparently in secular decline, and the left's critics eager to prove that its energies are dissipated and that it is destined to go the way of Poujadism, anarcho-syndicalism and absolute monarchy into the dustbin of history, this has become one of the central questions of modern politics.

What is really at issue is whether the decline of the left, both as movement and as sensibility, is cyclical or secular.

For although its competitors are in such difficulty, so apparently unsure about which energies to capture and which to reject, it is the left which is experiencing the deepest political crisis. It alone seems to be facing imminent historical closure. Some of the causes, such as the effects of 1989 on the Marxist left, the discrediting of economic planning, the crises of state finance and the problems of adapting social democracy to a more integrated world economy are well rehearsed. But many of the causes if anything go deeper, in a malaise that is highlighted in the very structure of the argument with which many of those on the right and centre now proclaim the death of socialism.

According to this argument, the main political energies of the modern era are largely spent. Socialism is nothing more than the obsolete and archaic symptom of conflicts that have gone cold. Just as its rise was intimately linked to the rise to prominence of the industrial working class, so will its fall be just as inevitable and irresistible. Sociology (and here the argument sidesteps the vast industrial proletariats of India, Brazil, South Africa or Korea) dictates that the very factors which raised the left up now cast it down, leading it the way of constitutional monarchy: paid lip service for the sake of continuity, but to all intents and purposes irrelevant. No one will ever again announce, as the English liberal Sir William Harcourt did in the 1890s, that we are all socialists now. The advance of democracy, so it is claimed, is now much more about procedures and the constitution of open societies, than it is about ends such as equality. Instead, in a greying, prosperous and 'post-socialist' era, the world of politics will be left only with the relatively uninteresting questions of managing largely self-governing societies.

Perhaps the most interesting feature of this argument is that its structure is Marxian. The very confidence in historical inevitability which once intimidated retreating reactionaries is now used to mesmerize and browbeat the left. The Marxists who once loved nothing better than to declare the obsolescence of their opponents, the scientific incontestability of their own knowledge, or the irresistible social logic that would guarantee their victory, now find their own guns turned around.

It is hard to exaggerate just how ironic this turn of events is. The right is now using the single most discredited part of the Marxist structure: the claim that history is unilinear and determined, and that an era of energetic class conflict will be replaced by an era of classlessness and the 'administration of things'. Moreover, these claims are now being made in the face of a century's experience that should have undermined once and for all the idea that there is any simple relation between politics, class and sociology. We now know that there are simply too many exceptions to any rule: the peasant communist movements that 'should' have waited for the emergence of proletariats; robust conservative parties that long outlived the disappearance of the traditional classes from which they grew; strong social-democratic parties in the most middle-class European countries and a weak left in the American working class. All have shown that things are far more open, and far more a matter of history and culture, than the old theories ever allowed. As Einstein once said of politics, there are simply too many variables at work.

But the serious flaw of these arguments about the inevitability of the left's demise is not that they underestimate the extent to which the world is open, but rather that they fail to see the extent to which it is open within consistent parameters. Against the odds, European politics (and through its remarkably successful export of ideologies, the politics of the world) continues to distil into the three great traditions of conservatism, liberalism and socialism. These may sometimes be used as little more than flags of convenience, and they may sometimes be disguised under national, religious or technocratic rhetoric. They may be mixed in new combinations such as socialistic economics and conservative morality, but 200 years that have changed all societies beyond recognition have not changed this underlying structure of the political cosmos.

This is not a banal observation. It would greatly surprise a visitor from the 1890s that there have been no final victories or resolutions, no scientific proofs of one ideology over another: that even such a conservative society as Japan contains powerful communist and socialist parties, that even as permissively liberal a culture as California sustains a moralistic and authoritarian right and that even as socialistic a society as Sweden can be governed by conservatives.

Why do they all survive? Two reasons stand out. One is that, although politics now reaches far beyond the nation-state to embrace questions of lifestyle and sexuality, global survival and global power, no political project that has anything interesting to say about the central issues of public power can define itself except in the terms of these traditions. The role, limits and values of the state continue to be bitterly contested and no amount of experience seems finally to prove the virtues of one set of answers over another. But there is also a second reason. The longevity and renewability of the great currents of political life seem to owe less to irreversible trends of political economy, than to their ability to feed off fundamental experiences of human life, to offer enduring insights into human and social nature, and to articulate enduring fears and hopes that resonate within any modern society. They survive because what they say has a universal relevance, because each has the potential to strike a chord beyond its immediate political constituencies, and because, for this very reason, their competitors are never able to achieve a permanent hegemony.

Each tradition offers distinctive solutions to enduring problems. One concerns the legitimate role of the state. Conservatism has emphasized the role of the state as guarantor of order and continuity, and liberalism its minimal role in sustaining the conditions for individual freedom, while socialism has understood the state as a medium for a more moral society and for the liberation of suppressed individual potential.

A second concerns the relation of the individual to the community. Where conservatism sees the community weighing down as a restraint on unreliable human nature, and where liberalism rests on the self-contained individual and sees the community as nothing more than an aggregation of individuals, the socialist tradition has always seen the community as something positive and enabling.

A third concerns fear. Where conservatism has always tended to play on fears of change and disorder, and liberalism on fears of the state, socialism has always gained its strength from the universality of fears of economic insecurity and oppression.

A fourth concerns equality. Traditional conservatism has tended to emphasize the natural origins of inequality, liberalism the virtues of equality of opportunity, socialism the importance of more equal outcomes.

These clusters of principles may at certain times have only a tenuous link to the programmes of parties that call themselves conservative, liberal or socialist. Electoral realities rarely permit ideological purity. They may be mixed and matched in more or less convincing combinations. But it is next to impossible to construct a political programme that does not draw from one or all of these traditions. Look, for example, at the only recent challenger to traditional political movements, the green movement. On one level, issues like global warming have created a new kind of politics, linking intergovernmental decisions, personal lifestyle choices and politically imposed limits on the market. Yet whenever they have come close to real influence, the greens have found themselves divided on traditional lines: between reactionaries, libertarians and communitarians, or between those who would use market forces and those who would simply assert what they believe to be right regardless of individual or market sovereignty.

These fundamentals seem to persist even as the balance between the traditions continually shifts, and as dominant traditions create countervailing tendencies through their symptoms of failure, moral dissatisfaction and loss of balance. Moreover, through these cycles, the traditions remain resistant to the rules of proof that apply to other kinds of knowledge. Belief in the sociability of human nature, for example, can be neither proved nor disproved (despite the attempts of many on the left, such as Noam Chomsky, to prove the genetically innate nature of human sociability and morality, and contrary attempts to prove once and for all that people are nasty, selfish or violent). One of the reasons why de Tocqueville's comment, quoted at the beginning of this essay, is misleading even as it is acute, is precisely that even without ignorance there are good grounds for reinventing political wheels.

The only types of political knowledge that can be tested are the concrete forms which ideas take, not the ideas themselves. Where such forms are concerned, experience can irretrievably discredit claims. Pure monetarism in the first world, central planning in the second world and import substitution strategies in the third world are obvious examples. The important point, however, is that their failures are not fatal to the traditions from which they come, but are more like childhood illnesses: unpleasant and temporarily debilitating, but ultimately strengthening.

This resilience is clearly the key to the persistence of old traditions. Ironically, however, it is also why the left has had such trouble understanding its own greatest strengths and weaknesses, for Marxism traditionally took a very different view. If you believe in the strictly progressive character of history, old ideas are by definition obsolete, and ideas produced by one kind of society lose their relevance to another. As in the mechanistic world-view of the nineteenth century, all energies are subject to the Second Law of Thermodynamics' principle of irreversible exhaustion.

There can be no denying the power of this insight. Political discourse does change irreversibly and social realities do shape the character of political argument. But the insight is at best partial, and at worst destructive. Within the left it often bred contempt for those early years when socialism came out of nonconformism, millenarianism, radical economics and trade unionism, as a bubbling cauldron of arguments, running the gamut from Christian utopianism, through workerist syndicalism to progressive reformism. Such a rejection of an unscientific past was a handy tool for vilifying those like William Morris who made of socialism 'an all embracing theory of life' with 'an ethic and religion of its own': an answer to the question of how to live.

As a result, much that was best in the tradition was cast out, so that it is only now possible to see that the left's history is less a progression from idealism to science and from naïvety to rigour, than a steady accretion of different modes of thought many of which retain their relevance even when their original causes disappear. Some of the Chartist arguments, for example, are almost indistinguishable from constitutionalist arguments made 150 years later. Many of the ideas of the ethical socialists achieve a new resonance in a world where global survival depends on ethics and personal responsibility getting the better of self-interest. And even guild socialism gains new relevance as more occupations seek the identity of a craft or profession, in control of their skills and their ethos. Some 150 years (roughly two consecutive lifetimes) since the word 'socialism' first came into use, the tradition is far from dead. It remains a ready source of energy.

Where there has been a change in recent years is in our understanding of the difference between the enduring values of socialism, values which long predate its parties and movements, and the forms it took as it came to power at the high point of industrial society. It is now much easier to see how much the left was shaped by taking power just when bureaucratic, rational, mass organization was at its most dynamic. The deficiencies of the era of national state socialism which began at the end of World War I – a tendency to favour top-heavy and bureaucratic structures, devoid of any means to balance the state's own vested interests – are now beyond dispute. But what is less often noticed is the extent to which at that time the left sold short its own tradition and underestimated the importance of the ethical foundations on which the movement was built. By internalizing the determinist self-image of industrial society it deceived itself into believing that it was a scientific movement of inevitable progress, rather than a carrier of enduring ideas about how people should live and how societies should cohere.

The long overdue death of communism makes this clearer. It reveals once again the long pedigree, the breadth, depth and vitality of the left tradition. And it confirms that, despite the brilliant analyses of thinkers like Gramsci and Luxemburg, communism generated no real insights about how societies should be organized that were superior to those of the broader socialist tradition and the humanist and democratic currents from which both evolved. In every case where it offered a new rule for social organization, the new turned out to be wrong.

That history of schism is at an end, and the left is now a broader church – possibly less coherent, but certainly less divided. With the old divisions gone, and the renewable energy sources, the strengths of the tradition, clearly intact, the question now moves forward. What will turn out to be the great new energies of our times, the new sources the left will need to tap to move on? What will be the driving forces for change?

It is always unwise to predict, particularly where politics is concerned. But there are at least four broad movements, unleashings of energy, which seem unlikely to falter, even if they confront new obstacles and challenges.

Far and away the most important is the still sweeping movement of democracy across the world, from China to Brazil, Kazakhstan to Turkey. This movement, still in historical terms in its infancy, remains full of potential for the left because it is never only about procedures, but is also always about the justice of outcomes, the rights and wrongs of how people are treated. That is why once unleashed the energies of a democratic culture tend to be restlessly ethical and emotive, always throwing up new challenges to those in power.

The second, and closely related, source of new energy is the transition towards an era of human capital. The shift from merchant to industrial capital, and more recently to finance capital, is now on the edge of another epochal shift towards human capital: the resources of skill, ingenuity and creativity. This shift is taking place in the very heart of capitalist organization, yet resonates remarkably well with old ideas of co-operation, democratized workplaces and the rights of the producer to control over his or her work. For the left it means that there is a new chance to complete the unfinished business of bringing democracy into economic life: not, as before, as a fetter on capitalism, but rather as a way of removing the barriers to its future development.

The third source of energy is the continued expansion of demands on states, public bodies and transnational organizations to extend their responsibility. Despite a decade of apparent retreat, the long history of expansion which gave the left such momentum earlier in the century has not been arrested. If anything, the shift towards more developed operations and towards public powers at one remove from the state has cleared the way for a new period of advance to solve the problems of ageing societies and environmental adaptation. The sheer intensity of a packed planet that makes individualism attractive also makes collectivism necessary.

The fourth set of energies is less immediately tangible but none the less important for that. The predictions of Marx, Keynes and others of a post-materialist world beyond scarcity may have been premature, but they were not necessarily wrong. In the prosperous societies of the first world, consumption looks unlikely to prove a very secure foundation for identity and self-realization. People inevitably look elsewhere: to family or work, to the communities in which they live, and to the needs of the planet as a whole. As a result, there are already signs that the political world is set to move beyond the emancipatory imperative on which socialism and liberalism often found common ground, towards more difficult questions about how to live, questions of being and purpose that can rarely be solved by individuals in isolation.

With life expectancy now thirty-five years longer in the west than it was at the beginning of the century, it is probably inevitable that people will take a more cautious, responsible and long-term view than they once did. Politics may indeed lose something of its youthful passion. but it is not likely to be in any way less concerned with questions of judgement and ethics. It seems more likely that the teenage scribblers who for 200 years have feverishly declared the end of history, ideology, capitalism, God and now socialism will go out of fashion, leaving the rest of us with the enduring questions: how to balance the needs of the individual and society; how to define the limits and responsibilities of the state; and how to define the nature of right and wrong in public life. For the left it will be an ability to offer a distinctive, relevant and enduring set of answers to these questions, and not any monopoly of scientific truth, that will guarantee a place at the heart of political life.

DEMOCRACY BEYOND SOVEREIGNTY: THE SHAPE OF A POSTMODERN WORLD ORDER

The world is a short way along a long path. As such, it can be hard to see what is important and what peripheral, to disentangle what is irreversible and what is cyclical. Nevertheless in this essay we want to make two very simple arguments. The first is that recent human history has seen an unmistakable trend towards making the peoples of the world, both separately and together, sovereign over their destinies. The second is that this sovereignty knows no obvious bounds, and that its expansive nature is bringing a quite new set of possibilities and problems on to the international stage.

Underlying these arguments are two parallel sets of transformations. The first is the spread of democracy. The slow democratic revolution, which arguably began in 1776 and 1789 and was given new momentum by the revolutions of 1848, 1870, 1917, 1945 and 1989 is continuing to transform the conduct of international affairs. As in earlier phases, new swathes of the world's peoples are being brought into the realm of politics: the great decisions about whom to govern and how, whom to fight and whom to befriend, that were once the privileged preserve of a handful of people. Today, even amid apparent retreats to irredentism and chauvinism, the long-term trend is unmistakably towards the sovereignty of an embryonic world public.

The second set of transformations has been about physical space. The traditional notion of sovereignty concerned control over territory. It arguably reached its apogee less than a lifetime ago when, with the exceptions of the Arctic and Antarctic, the whole world was for the first time enclosed within national boundaries. At first this seemed to make each area of land a private fiefdom. Today, however, it is apparent that this was just a step on the road towards a shared sovereignty over all physical space exercised, albeit through many different forms, at a global level. In the military sphere this has become most apparent in the negotiations of the world's greatest military powers to establish shared systems of mutual surveillance and oversight to prevent war. In economics it has resulted in new policing powers exercised by global bodies such as the IMF and GATT. Politically, its sharpest edge is the simple fact that environmental survival requires that national rights to act within national borders are overridden.

These twin transformations, the one about the subjects of international affairs, the other about its domain, are together transforming the meaning of sovereignty. They are both fragmenting it and contributing to its reformation at a new level. As such, they are adding new layers to the already complex meaning of sovereignty. At its simplest, to be sovereign, whether as a consumer, a citizen or a nation, means to be autonomous and beyond compulsion. It means being above all other institutions or persons. This is its core meaning, shared by a range of different traditions, and present when sovereignty was first used to describe an attribute of the state. As defined by Jean Bodin, it referred then to the central monopoly within any nation, the 'absolute and perpetual power over the citizens and subjects', a monopoly held by kings, dictators and parliaments. It is a monopoly of authority (even if not always of power), an aspiration to total control through law and institutions over a defined territory. It embodies the idea that all relevant power can be concentrated in a single legitimate point, and held by a single person or institution.

This idea of monopoly, first of force, second of law, and often also of culture and knowledge, first developed in Europe before being exported to define a world system of nation-states, each

internally monopolist of political and legal authority, and able
to negotiate with other like bodies. The peculiar features of
European states, their centralization of power, their administrative
structures, their attempts at rational legitimation and their mass
armies, subsequently became the properties demanded of any
participant in the world system. The same was true of their
concept of complete power within the territory, a sharply different
conception to the multiple layers of obligation familiar in the
medieval world.

The states system, which evolved between the sixteenth and
nineteenth centuries, can be said to have constituted the first
modern 'order of sovereignty': a system of nation-states of clear
territorial boundaries and varying degrees of absolutism within
them. Defined in Pufendorf's *De systematibus civitatum*' in 1675,
and more recently by Martin Wight and others, the foundation
of the system was independent political authorities 'which recognize no superior',[1] but which recognize the same claim to independence of all the other members of the state system. Paralleled in
some respects by earlier states systems, unique in others, this
system turned out over time to be rigorously competitive. It
sharpened up the skills of states, their military technologies and
economic capacities, so well as to assist them in dominating the
world, first by sea and later by land.

The basis of this order was transformed by the American and
French revolutions. From then on democrats asserted that it was
in fact the people, and not the king, who should be sovereign.
Their will should prevail over all others, constituting the monopoly of legitimate power within the boundaries of the nation.
According to this view, popular sovereignty and national sovereignty were but two sides of the same coin, the internal and
external dimensions of a homogeneous entity of which the state
was an expression.

This model of a democratic national sovereignty has taken a
long time to prevail. Indeed, it is only at the very end of the
twentieth century that the last refuges of absolutism, and the last
states claiming authority beyond their national communities, have
succumbed to this idea. Only now has foreign affairs been democratized in these countries, and only now is it becoming impossible

for governments either to carry out diplomacy without regard to the values and sympathies of their people, or to protect them from the views of others. As a result, many have interpreted the end of the cold war as the culmination of the long struggle to implement what is now an old dream of a world system made up of sovereign, democratic states. Seeing the world as potentially rule based and drawing on a sanguine view of history, they argue that this order is stable and robust: indeed, it is not only a realistic description of the world, but also the best of all possible worlds.

This view has created a new divide between opposing ways of viewing the world. It directly mirrors the way that democratic theory divides into two schools of thought, each drawing on a distinct meaning inherent in the etymology of the word. For one, the essence of democracy is a set of transparent and commonly agreed rules for decision making, rules that are designed to protect minority views, and to safeguard negative freedoms. According to the second view, democracy is rule by the people, the assertion of their values and interests in order to expand positive freedoms, without external (or constitutional) limitation.

Proceduralism

Applied to international relations, these two approaches generate very different perspectives. At present the first, the proceduralist school, has a much more coherent account of the state of the world. For its proponents, the defining feature of the democratization process has been the victory of liberal ideals in both the political and market spheres. Liberal theories of society have been extrapolated to the international stage, which is seen as a global society made up of separate individual components. These components are states which group with other states, often on a regional level, acting within a Kantian rational international legal framework in the pursuit of their interests. In theory, all can act with perfect freedom, but within a set of laws as well as a set of shared values and assumptions internationally agreed and policed. Those who transgress the rules of the international community will be punished by that community. A set of procedures are in place –

supported by all – for collective decision making: where necessary, too, there are the means of enforcing these rules.

The aim of the system is to protect the autonomy of each individual actor, their ability to live, to trade freely and to communicate. States are to be as free as possible on the international stage so long as their freedom does not invade the freedom of others. Within states the same rules, constitutive of liberal society, are applied, but this time at the level of the individual. The state of advance of a system can be judged by the extent to which it leaves the individual free, and by the extent to which it constrains the powerful to the same laws which apply to the powerless. Because the model posits similar structures for the internal organization of states and for the organization of the world as a whole, it is a universal model, applying universal principles of law and autonomy to all layers of social organization.

The advocates of this view would argue that what we are now witnessing are problems of transition – both internal and external. Pre-democratic, pre-liberal states like Iraq or Serbia engage in aggressions because both in their external and internal structures they have yet to be brought into the liberal world. The absence of a liberal-democratic polity makes speculative aggressions possible, while the absence of a fully developed international legal order makes it possible to believe that aggressions will go unpunished. In the same way, the problems of resurgent nationalism and ethnic tensions in Eastern Europe and the former Soviet Union will last only until stable democratic nations are formed, which can then be slotted into the structure of the world order. In other words, underlying the argument is a claim that there is an inherent connection between democracy, liberal proceduralism and mutual respect. In support of this view it is often pointed out that democracies never launch aggressive wars, and that the experience of law-based society at home sustains acceptance of laws at an international level.

This thesis has profound implications. If correct, if implies that the world is capable of moving in a fairly short period of time beyond the use of force as a common tool for resolving disputes. It implies that a single model is transferable throughout the world, in all cultures, and that a world society of common rules is immanent.

The second model begins with a critique of the first. It sees democracy as much less inherently pacific. It points to the many examples of democracies launching wars, although for reasons we shall come to, few examples of them launching unpopular ones. The USA, for example, has sponsored invasions of Guatemala, Panama, Grenada, Cuba, Vietnam and Cambodia. Long after the introduction of universal suffrage, countries like Britain and France were involved in wars, not all of them explicable as part of a process of decolonization. Indeed, what is striking about the modern age is the connection not between democracy and peace, but between the fact of international hegemony and a certain kind of populist (and usually democratically sanctioned) imperialism, as was the case in Britain in the 1880s, and the USA in the 1940s and 1950s.

The proceduralist position is equally vulnerable to the fact that several of the leading democracies have blithely ignored the decisions of international organizations where these appeared to conflict with national interest (the US response to International Court rulings over the bombing of Nicaraguan harbours is just one example). Many democracies have been selective in their acceptance of international judgements and jurisdictions such as those of the European Court of Human Rights. In a range of different cases – from extraditions to espionage activities – international laws, which lack policing mechanisms, have been routinely overridden.

These exceptions cannot be brushed aside. They are crucial because the real test of any world order, or indeed of any system of laws, is its ability to constrain the powerful from abusing this power. Laws that can only back decisions with the accord of the most powerful lack credibility. The key question is the old one of *quis custodiet custodios*, yet the rational legal order appears unable to answer it.

The second democratic model, the ideal of rule by the people with minimum impediment, offers an alternative answer to this question: its answer is that a self-conscious global public can over time become the sovereign entity overriding the self-interest of states and exercising direct influence over the public opinion of dominant nations. Where the first model is confined to the mutual respect of sovereign nations, the latter is at ease with publics that exist across national boundaries and with intervention in the internal affairs of other nations. Where the first is built on an agglomeration of rules, the means of resolving problems, the second is organized around ends and is less scrupulous (or pedantic) about how they are to be achieved.

The agent of this older meaning of democracy in the modern world is that amorphous thing, public opinion. It is not without significance that within nations even the most autocratic power has to take account of the shifting moods of public opinion, which may infect its armies, its civil servants and its capacity to rule. In the same way, if there is any discipline on the actions of states, it is now as likely to come from an international public opinion, organized by the media and non-state organizations, and spreading over into the domestic publics of most of the major countries, as to come simply from rules: or rather, to be more precise, rules are only likely to be implemented if backed by a democratic will, by a political rather than a purely legal legit-imacy. It is this community of values and peoples that arguably counts for more than any association of nations, just as it did in the past. As Herbert Butterfield wrote in relation to earlier states systems, 'the effective forces making for some sort of combination may be the elements of an antecedent common culture'.[2]

However, unlike a legal machine, this community of values, or rather a mosaic of overlapping communities, is, like all democrac-ies, far from rational. It is capable of combining irrationality, prejudice, unethical behaviour and unprovoked aggression. Democratization, whether within nations or across boundaries, brings different (and competing) cultures, national and ethnic prejudices, sympathies and ethics. It draws on the various growing international communities, whether of professional middle classes, of business, of the new age and green movements, of Jews or Palestinians, Catholics or Muslims. It feeds off their growing confidence and assertiveness, which are not generally easing the transition to a rational law-based model. Instead they tend to raise difficult choices on to the world stage of diplomacy: issues such as AIDS, global warming or migration, aid or population control, that are far less resolvable and far more multidimensional than those of traditional diplomacy.

Indeed, where there are consistent tendencies in democracy across the world, these are not reinforcing a rational and procedural world system, a Grotian world of international law, but rather tending to undermine the subject of the proceduralists' case – the nation-state – and thus the whole notion of a global nation-state system. As citizens find themselves receivers of decisions made within other polities (such as a nuclear plant on the border or an interest rate rise in a stronger economy), and as they demand more porous boundaries whether for goods, travel or information, their sense of political horizons seems to grow. Their desire to exercise sovereignty as individuals or communities can no longer be contained within the representative forms of the nation-state.

As a result, the transformation of the old idea of international relations as a mutual contract of non-intervention, a process that can be said to have begun with the UN Charter's emphasis on the preservation of peace, the European convention's assertion of collective enforcement, and the Nuremberg Tribunal's assertion of higher laws than those of the nation-state, is entering a new era, as an embryonic global public searches for an appropriate form of sovereignty.

The Third Phase

This is what is at stake in what we want to call the third phase of sovereignty, successor to the first era of absolutism and the second of popular national sovereignty. Ours is an age of democratizing international relations and spreading transparency that can be understood only as an evolution both of other processes of democratization in warfare, communication and the economy, and of a profound deterritorialization of human activity.

War is a good starting point, since it is the point where sovereignty is most clearly put to the test. During the first phase of sovereignty, war was the prerogative of the monarch, or indeed of narrowly based parliaments, to be carried out purely according to the dictates of national interest. Over the course of the last two centuries, however, the nature of warfare has been completely transformed. The colossal armies of Napoleonic France and World War I Europe required mass mobilization, mass propaganda and, above all, what Walter Lippman called the manufacture of consent. Unpopular wars became unwinnable wars. For the same reasons, within boundaries it has become increasingly hard for small cliques or armies to seize and hold power. From Iran and Poland to the Philippines and Moscow, people power has defeated armies from within. Even with the smaller professional armies of the late twentieth century, war has become limited and even defined by public relations, fought on news screens as well as battlefields. With tactics shaped by the dictates of television and the unpredictable nature of public emotion, this has dramatically limited the room for manoeuvre of the governments of powerful nations; indeed, war can no longer be conceived either as a tool of statecraft, or as a direct relationship between two or more nations. Like a Freudian superego sharing the bed with two lovers, world opinion is always present even on the most distant battlefield.

But war has also been taken out of the control of traditional sovereignty in other ways.[3] The recent wave of arms agreements has been based on principles of mutual surveillance, joining the de facto surveillance of satellites with de jure rights to send observers to even the most secret missile site. This is only one massive breach of the traditional rules of sovereignty, for there are also other ways in which the nature of war has shifted. Few wars are now defined by territorial integrity: most are undertaken either as joint international exercises or as quasi-civil wars, rather than as classical conflicts between nation-states. Their tactics, too, are generally at one remove from classical conceptions. Indeed, with 'vertically mobile' missiles and helicopter-borne troops, warfare concentrates on key nodes of networks of transport, communication or energy, rather than the territories in between, or on transterritorial ventures such as the US raid on

Libya, anti-drugs initiatives in South America or the Iraqi attacks on Israel during the Gulf War.

So even if the technologies of war have taken it further from direct popular control, the technologies of communication have brought it back. Today anyone with a television or radio is as well informed about wars or coups as the great majority of foreign services, and many more have the intellectual, informational and time resources to develop sophisticated opinions. Just as the spread of democracy through nations would have been inconceivable without national media, primarily print, to develop public opinion and a sense of civil society, and to foster a distinctive national high culture, so is the emergence of global democracy inconceivable without communications: international news services, satellite broadcasting, world radio services, a culture that permeates borders with cassette tapes and videos, and lingua francas, above all English, that help to make mental and physical borders porous. As electronic communication becomes decisive in economic and social life, displacing traditional community and face-to-face relationships, things which can be communicated become vital – not only such things as facts, prices and forecasts which drive world markets, but also much softer things such as trust, empathy and ideas.

One dimension of this power was seen during the failed Soviet coup of August 1991. Even surrounded by tanks the Russian parliament was still able to communicate by fax; even under house arrest President Gorbachev remained in touch through the BBC World Service. Both survived at least in part because of the hostility of the world media to their opponents, but also because of a sense, however tenuous, of solidarity between the people on the streets of Moscow and those in the living rooms around the world. In China too, after Tiananmen Square, soldiers were posted on every fax machine to stop them being used to mobilize world opinion, correctly recognizing that this posed a potentially greater threat than any physical insurrection.

In so doing, the Chinese authorities came up against the third element in this story of democratization, for in so far as they cut off communications they also cut off economic dialogue, and thus the very economic prosperity on which they had come to depend. Whereas in the past an economic opening could be negotiated by a handful of senior officials, and contained to a relatively small area, participation in the world economy today requires the direct involvement of hundreds of thousands if not millions as partners, managers, translators and designers, all engaged in a multitude of transactions which cannot be efficiently channelled through any one point.

Such participation means being involved in a deterritorialized economy, with hierarchies of power quite distinct from those of the nation-state. The logic of markets serving sovereign consumers is to spread territorially in order to find new markets, new sources of labour and new materials. Rational organization is blind to jurisdiction. States, by contrast, seek to control economic activity within territories, and can clearly not do this if their boundaries are wholly open.[4] As they have conflicted, however, it has generally been the market that has prevailed. Traditional notions of national comparative advantage and control over territory have been eroded by the electronic movement of currency, equities and invoices, and by the fact that in an open market it is simply not possible to define ownership and production by their nationality.[5] The dematerialization of economics has also been significant. In international competition, concern with physically located natural resources is a sign of backwardness, concern with levels of skill, invention and productivity the sign of advance.[6] Taken together, these various changes tend to mean that the relations of states – and their populations – with global transnational companies are now in many respects more important than relations between states.

War, communication and economy have all been wrested away from traditional sovereign powers by the ease with which money, information and weapons can be moved. But it is the movement of people that is if anything most decisive in now threatening the second age of sovereignty as much as the first. Freedom of movement aided by transport technology, a freedom that is used by millions as never before to travel for work or pleasure, is inherently at odds with the sovereignty of peoples who are members of a community within defined boundaries. Historians report far greater movements of people in antiquity than was previously recognized, but it is only in the modern age that truly large-scale population movements became possible: the global spread first of the peoples of the colonizing nations and, under coercion, of their slaves; the mass migrations such as that from Eastern Europe to North America; the spread of the Jewish and Palestinian diasporas; the migration of Americans and later Japanese behind their investments; the vast movements of East Europeans westwards, North Africans northwards; all have ruptured the nineteenth century ideal of the homogeneous nation, content within its boundaries, and all have called into question what are the qualifications for participation in popular sovereignty within any nation.

When people move they become threats to nation-states. It is not only the totalitarian regimes which buttressed their sovereignty by preventing the movement of people, and were in turn brought down by movements of people. According to J. Bhagwati, 'there is practically universal agreement among modern states that free flows of human beings, no matter how efficacious for world efficiency, should not be permitted'.[7] Personal autonomy, the right not only to exit but also to enter other countries, is simply at odds with the pre-democratic rules of membership of nations. Within months of the collapse of the Iron Curtain, a new and less visible curtain had been erected to hold back the thousands wanting to take advantage of economic opportunities in the West.

The experience of the twentieth century is that most barriers are at best temporary. Barriers to the movement of money, ideas and even missiles have been progressively chipped away. Much the same may happen with people, as has already proved the case in the Mediterranean or on the USA–Mexico border. Flows of unarmed people can count for more than flows of armed people, as the East Germans showed when their civilian population became a greater threat to West German security after the collapse of the Berlin Wall than their army had ever been. But the effect of a more mobile population may turn out to be a more paradoxical one from the point of view of sovereignty. In order to prevent flows of people, powerful nations are driven to take some responsibility for the economic security of their weaker neighbours, to cede sovereignty in exchange for stability. Most significant of all, however, is the fact that such policies can only be justified through a language of common interest which transcends the narrow national interest that could be met through coercive means. In other words, in order to protect their boundaries they have to concede the very foundational idea of the nation, the idea of a definable interest common to all members of the nation but to no others.

These four sets of factors, the military, the communicational, the economic and the human, help to explain why our language for understanding world affairs needs to adapt, and why the opening and democratization of international relations cannot easily be cast into the hopeful frames of an earlier age. The next stage of the argument therefore concerns the key actors on this changing world stage, and the character of the arguments which will define them.

Our analysis emphasizes the crucial role of communication in defining the nature of the emerging forms of sovereignty. It suggests three types of critical actor.

(1) The first is the diplomat. It has become a commonplace that the task of modern diplomats and embassies is scarcely analogous to that of their predecessors. Many of the same technologies that helped to foster a dynamic democratic opinion, the national press and the telegraph, also fatally undermined the traditional role of the diplomat. Five thousand years of human history, when diplomacy was carried out by a professional cadre according to the precepts of national or dynastic interest, came to an end, as the diplomat became little more than an emissary for decisions taken in a distant capital according to the dictates of democratic opinion. This erosion of diplomacy continued throughout the twentieth century as the telegraph was succeeded by the telephone and more recently by the proliferation of multiple sources of intelligence (media, banks, specialist organizations), often with superior analysis to that offered by the professionals.

Surprisingly, however, the further democratization of international relations beyond sovereign states gives a new lease of life to the diplomat. The best diplomat becomes an actor in public opinions: explaining domestic opinion to publics in other states and vice versa, often on television or in print; brokering coalitions not only of governments but also of non-government organizations; negotiating almost always multilaterally and in more than one dimension, linking economy and ecology, finance and might, and often becoming a partisan for common global interests within the domestic state. Increasingly, the most important task of the diplomat is open communication to public opinions, in place of closed communication to government decision makers; communication to clarify, to simplify, to remove misunderstanding.

This may prove an immensely difficult task, for the most legitimate fear of a further democratization of world relations is that the media and the public are simply not up to the demands which will be placed on them. The *polis* may simply be becoming too large and complex for meaningful participation in decisions. As John Dunn put it, 'the Athenian demos could, despite Plato, understand the main outlines of what it was being asked. Consider today by contrast the nature of decision on energy policy, the regulation of international trade or the design and deployment of weapons systems'.[8]

(2) The second set of players will be those who can articulate a common ethics. Within nations democratic argument has sometimes been rational, but it has at other times been emotive, chauvinistic and myopic. Arguments for self-interest have no inherently stronger pull than arguments about identity, about ethics or about community. At a global level, we should expect the same mix with, in the age of televisual politics, even less time to reflect than is possible in national politics. Some types of state behaviour will be prohibited, probably well beyond extremes such as genocide and the sponsorship of terrorism. Some modest economic redistribution will be acceptable (although within severe limits: altruism tends to be very price sensitive), and some types of public interest action will seem as natural as they do within boundaries.

If we begin to see the embryo of a single global community conscious of a common interest and common values, the 'priestly' political leaders who can articulate ethical ideas may become increasingly significant. Those who took on evangelical roles, subordinating narrow national self-interest to wider interests (obvious and opposite examples might include Jimmy Carter and Fidel Castro) may prove to be harbingers of the future as much as the professional negotiators and technocrats. With their help, universal values may spread alongside localized ones, rooted in the experiences of different communities which may only rarely coincide with state boundaries.[9] Out of such a burgeoning dialogue, a mosaic of interests and ethics, the proceduralist vision of a world law may well emerge. But all historical example suggests that the culture must precede the institutions for them to succeed. Constitutions come after revolutions not before them. Moreover, as is the case within nations, new global constitutional arrangements may well have to await the same kinds of crisis and disaster that have so often proven decisive in creating a culture for change.

(3) The third set of players will be the institutions which seek to crystallize the interests and values of the emerging global constituency. These may not be the direct descendants of the cluster of bodies that evolved after 1945, for with a stronger international democratic civil society, many international organizations may find it hard to remain legitimate unless they too can prove their democratic credentials, and unless they can find a *modus vivendi* with a panoply of non-government bodies. This will surely prove difficult. Much of the United Nations was organized as a top-heavy bureaucracy, designed above all to respect the self-esteem of national governments. Efficiency and outputs had almost no weight in its decision-making processes. Voting systems bore little relationship to global opinion, whether in the form of one nation, one vote (which equalizes China and the Comores) at the United Nations, or in the form of the one dollar, one vote principles of the IMF and World Bank.

But probably more important than voting procedures themselves will be the other rules of oversight and conduct that ensure open and accountable governance. For institutions created at the apogee of state administration such changes will be hard. Institutions like the UN are not inherently well suited for adaptation to an era when states will again be lean rather than expansive, strategic rather than operational. But if, against expectations, they do begin to make that transition, we should expect to see a quite new panoply of democratic forms: public hearings on major decisions; transparency over actions and decision-making procedures; independent audits and balancing powers; devolution of operations according to principles of contract from a strategic core, in place of appointments in spoils systems; all measures which will be essential if bodies necessarily far removed from the scrutiny of public opinion are to remain effective and legitimate.

Their incentive to achieve such self-discipline may be greater if, as is likely, there is competition from below, such as supranational democratic approaches outside the international institutions, moving from the international scrutiny of elections to the international staging of elections. It is not hard to imagine such things as referenda beyond national boundaries; self-created global parliaments of particular groups, religions or interests; continental parliaments representing their national counterparts on the model of the European Parliament, all jostling for legitimacy and power, and the attention of the media, and all seeking to capture some part of the fragmenting sovereignties of dozens of nation-states.

Beyond Sovereignty

Sovereignty was once the foundation of the international order, and the point where domestic politics met international realities. Its sway is now under threat not only in terms of juridical authority, where there is general agreement that states can have obligations under international law and that world moods of public opinion have a standing of their own, but also in the sense that few states can exercise meaningful control over their own affairs. The deterritorialization of capital, information, opinions and war have combined to undermine the very notion of sovereignty: a monopoly of public power within defined territories, able to negotiate with other similar monopolies. Instead, world powers are beginning, bilaterally, multilaterally or even without any state sanction, to exercise power across boundaries and regardless of traditional sovereignty.

Since, as Niklas Luhman has pointed out, 'the state is the formula for the self-description of the political system of society',[10] the failure to provide an adequate description of what states are for and how they should deal with other states has proved profoundly unsettling for politics as a whole. It has played a not inconsiderable role in the wider crisis of politics and the rise of a new antipolitical ethos. Just as the economy and technology have now transcended the forms in which they developed, so is the democracy which grew up around the nation-state, organized around parties, national media and institutions, now bursting its banks like a huge river flooding out across a plain in search of new channels to follow.

Notes

1   Adam Watson, *The Evolution of International Society*, Routledge, London, 1992, p. 3.
2   Herbert Butterfield, in H. Butterfield and M. Wight (eds), *Diplomatic Investigations*, Allen and Unwin, London, 1966, p. 13.
3   Susan Strange and John Stopford, *Rival States, Rival Firms: competition for world market shares*, Cambridge University Press, Cambridge, 1991.
4   R. Gilpin, *The Political Economy of International Relations*, Princeton University Press, Princeton, 1987, p. 11.
5   Robert Reich, *The Work of Nations*, Simon and Schuster, London, 1991.
6   P. Cerny, *The Changing Architecture of Politics*, Sage, London, 1990.
7   J. Bhagwati, 'Incentives and disincentives: international migration', *Weltwirtschaftliches Archiv*, 120(4), p. 680.
8   John Dunn, *Interpreting Political Responsibility*, Polity, Cambridge, 1990,
9   See Charles B. Beitz, 'Sovereignty and morality in international affairs', in D. Held (ed.), *Political Theory Today*, Polity, Cambridge, 1991.
10 Niklas Luhman, *Political Theory in the Welfare State*, De Gruyter, New York, 1990.

Index